AFRICATOWN OMOTUNDE MURAL

35000 YEARS OF AFRICAN HISTORY

Order this book online at
www.centreakanga.com
info@africatowncdc.org

This book is published in conjunction with
Africatown Omotunde Mural, the mural street museum at Kidd Park Swimming Pool, Africatown-Plateau, Mobile, Alabama, by artist mural designer from Benin-Cameroon, Jeki ESSO, an initiative of ACDC, Africatown Community Development Corporation.
Unveiling of the Africatown Omotunde Mural took place at the Kidd Park Celebration, on Africatown Community Day, on June 24, 2023 (Year 6259 of Ancient African calendar).

Published by Dagan Éditions & Dagan Panafrican Press Group
Africatown CDC
P.O. Box 535 Mobile, AL 36601
info@africatowncdc.org | 251-355-ACDC (2232)
https://www.africatowncdc.com/

Historical advisor: Dr Koabena Dieudonne Gnammankou
Editorial assistance by Dr Irma McClaurin
Special thanks to Dr Gnammankou for the photos

ISBN : 978-2-919612-99-4

Distributors: ACDC, Africatown Artifacts and Akanga Cultural Center
https://centreakanga.com/
sales@daganpanafricanpress.com
info@africatowncdc.org | 251-355-ACDC (2232)

Printed in the United States

CONTENTS

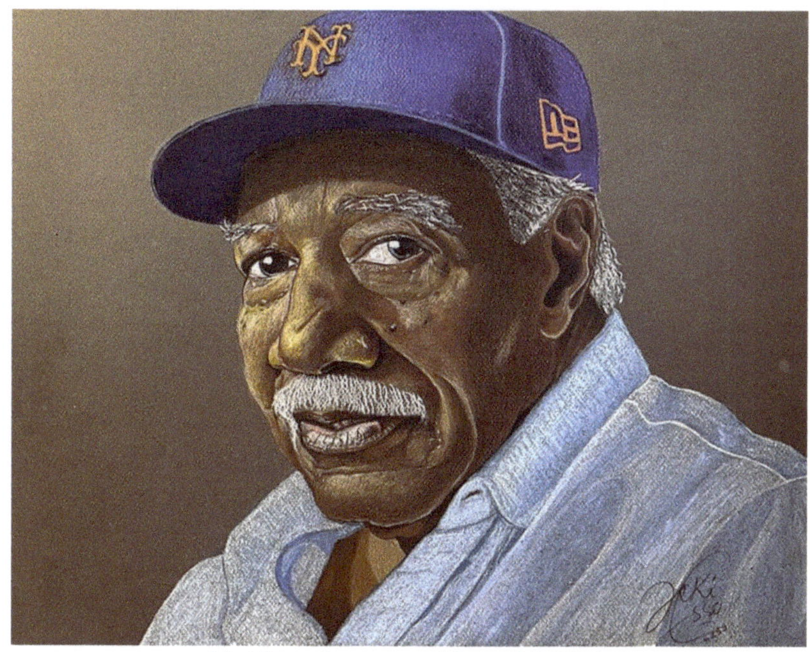

Mr Cleon Jones, president of ACDC

AFRICATOWN COMMUNITY DEVELOPMENT CORPORATION (ACDC)

Our Mission

To preserve and celebrate the history and culture of Africatown and the resilience of its residents.

To restore and expand the beauty, livability and sustainability of its neighborhoods.

To improve the roles and quality of education at the Mobile County Training School.

Contact: www.africatowncdc.org
info@africatowncdc.org
P.O. Box 535
Mobile, AL 36601
251-355-ACDC (2232)

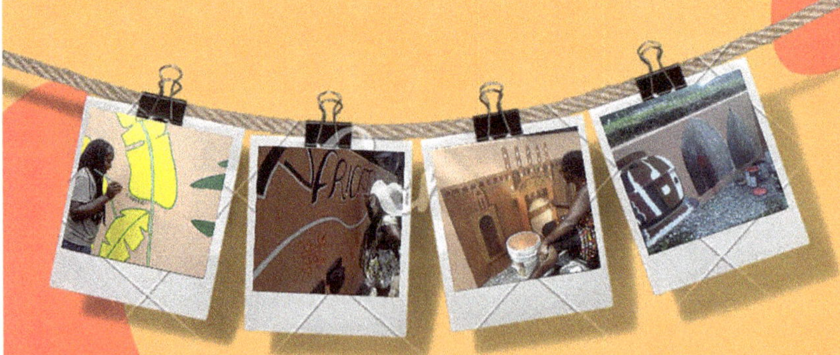
ACDC invites you at the community
Grand Opening
THE HERITAGE WALL,
KIDD PARK IN AFRICATOWN
Saturday, June 24th 9:30 am

Preface

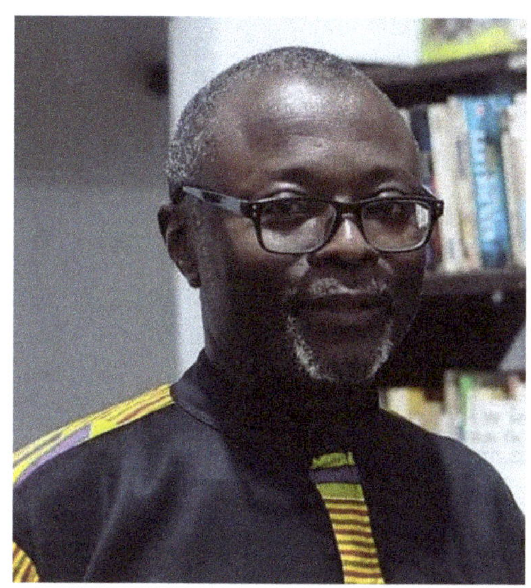

From the mural to the printed book and the digital book!
What a joy to be able to preface this beautiful book that you hold in your hands!
I am always amazed by the magic of drawing, illustration or painting. The artist-painter is a creator, a demiurge.

After the domestication of the verb, speech and languages, the first men and women invented graphic abstraction in Africa. Our very distant African ancestors who used varieties of pigments of several colors dating from 350,000 to 400,000 years ago - discovered by Lawrence Braham in 1993 - in Zambia at Twin Rivers Kopje near Lusaka, are at the origin of Art and symbolic thought.

And the rock art that was developed over tens of thousands of years almost everywhere on the continent - Cradle of Humanity, is an "incomparable documentary source".

As the eminent Malian researcher Jacques Habib Sy puts it so well, *in L'Afrique, berceau de l'écriture (Africa, cradle of writing)*, L'Harmattan, 2014, "the images left by prehistoric man for posterity remain the first open book of natural history and art, and undoubtedly, the first signs which precede the writing…".

In Benin, we have preserved the artistic and graphic tradition of bas-reliefs on the walls of the former royal palaces of Agbome and also on the walls of the Vodoun convents in Ouidah, Porto-Novo and elsewhere. Professor Noureini Tidjani-Serpos, founder of a private museum in the capital of Benin (Musée Abdou Tidjani-Serpos), aptly calls the murals and walls of bas-reliefs the Street Museums.

In several regions of West and South Africa, the mural painting of dwellings has remained a feminine activity for generations, as the mural designer Jeki Esso shows us in her imposing and magnificent fresco of almost 40 meters, which was unveiled in 2023 in Africatown, and whose photos make up this book. Her work builds on the feminine decorative artistic tradition that is far from disappearing among Kassena women (in Burkina Faso, Ghana) and Ndebele (South African Republic) for example.

Ancient Africa, the Africa of the great kingdoms and empires, Africa before European trafficking in African war captives to America, the Africa of science and technology, its monumental architecture that we tend to forget, its systems of thought and concepts, its art and culture, its symbols, the art of African living and perceiving the world, are all themes that the artist Jeki Esso has immortalized in her creation. This mural of Africatown that the ACDC Association commissioned will be a major element of reconnection for the populations of Africatown, Africky Town. In Fongbe, a national language of Benin, we would say Afriki-To. "To" means the city or the country.

Through this mural, Jeki Esso offers a permanent African presence in such a beautiful way to Africatown, in an ideal location that is a public place intended for youth, the Kidd Mural Pool.

The artist, who is my wife, accompanied me to the United States as part of my year as resident researcher and Fulbright visiting professor at the University of South Alabama. She often replied to those who asked her what she was doing in the United States that she was on sabbatical from her position as director of the Center de Cultures Akanga in Porto-Novo in Benin, and that she had come for sightseeing. Jeki could not have imagined that by volunteering to participate in the mural, to make herself useful to the community of Africatown who welcomed us so well, she would leave deep marks in this other Africa. She never imagined the profound impact and the symbolic importance of this artistic work. The day she finished her mural, a history teacher from Colorado who came to photograph the mural told her that she had chosen Jeki Esso's Africatown Omotunde Mural as the theme for her pedagogy workshop "Teach Africatown" as part of the National Endowment for the Humanities (NEH) Landmarks. Gorgeous, right?

But from a symbolic point of view, as Jeki started working on the mural, the most emotional moment was the day when I showed her a page from Sylviane Diouf's book, Dreams of Africa in Alabama, page where the author had published the list of African names of 50 of the 110 victims of the crime against humanity (enslavement) that was the despicable historical trafficking in human beings.

Among the 110 surviving Africans of the Middle passage out of the 125 transported by force in the slave ship Clotilde from Ouidah to Mobile, Alabama in 1860 (fifty years after slavery was declared illegal and ended), a man or a woman bore the name "ESSO". The same name as Jeki ESSO…

Koabena Dieudonné Gnammankou, Ph.D., Fulbright visiting professor and scholar-in-residence, University of South Alabama and Africatown
Université de Abomey-Calavi
Scientific Director, Akanga Cultural Center, Porto-Novo, (www.centreakanga.com)
Director, DAGAN Editions

Award winning author for his famous book, *Abraham Hanibal, Prince of Logone. Pushkin's African Ancestor*, Books of Africa London, 2015, translated from French (*Abraham Hanibal, l'aïeul noir de Pouchkine*, Présence Africaine, 1996).

Introduction

Art that Makes Sense

This fresco is named OMOTUNDE. It is the sixth I have produced--there are three in France, indoors, and two in Benin, outdoors. To date, this is the largest one I have painted.

You may wonder why a mural? It began with an idea from the Africatown Community Development Corporation (ACDC), located in Africatown, Plateau, Alabama. They wanted images of Africa that would welcome people to Africatown. The mural is the first thing people see as they turn onto the road that leads into the community.

As an artist, I believe murals take the place of speech and serve to visually challenge passers-by and provide them with information that they might not have ordinarily seek out; admit it, when we are driving or evening walk, most of us are caught up in our daily preoccupations. Art stops us! It demands that we pause, slow down our brain, and makes us think what do those images mean, what do those symbols represent?

Omotunde is a Yoruba word that translates into "the child who returns home". In making this the name of the Africatown mural, I wanted to symbolically reconnect the people of Africatown with their African roots. The symbols, words, and images that I have used in the Omotunde mural serve to reconnect and reunite Africatown and its people with Africa and her people.

I am an African woman born in Cameroon and currently living in Benin. In addition to being an artist, author, and illustrator, I am also a singer, and have travelled to Europe and also the United States, but never in a capacity where I could connect with the people—with Black people.

Over this last year, I have had the opportunity to observe and participate in the culture and history of Africatown. What I have learned is that our African American family came from several parts of the continent, though we do not know exactly where. Given the lack of specificity about the ancestral origins of most African Americans, I wanted to create art that would give words, images, and patterns and connect the African American diaspora with all of their possible African roots.

I envisioned this mural, as a journey through 35,000 years of African history. The images, symbols, colors, writings are intended to remind the people of Africatown and other Americans of African descent who their ancestors really were. I wanted them to SEE Africa, which for most are just images from books and movies, and take pride in the enormous impact that Africa and African descended people have had all over the planet. Most people don't know that Africa contributed the first mathematical formulas, designed and built some of the most magnificent monumental structures, developed a powerful scientific spirituality that has resulted in the computer science that we use daily, had its own African philosophy before Plato and Aristotle, held an African vision of the world, and practiced African ways of life that promoted the sustainability of cultural transmission. I was confident that showing strong symbols and mathematical equations in the mural, , would be more telling than simply drawing the human forms. This mural is filled with the diversity of African cultures for it is a continent, not a single nation, but many different countries and cultures.

The mural is also an expression of community participation. As I designed the images and painted them, I was accompanied by the expertise of a wonderful team of men, Africatown residents, women and youth, who were accustomed to doing community work. Their support of me and my work reflects the African proverb, *It takes a village.*

Most of the time, the process of designing and painting the mural moved smoothly and went like clockwork. Other times, there were a hiccups and few challenges. The major one was the weather! This was my first time in Mobile, and I did not know what to expect—it was the unpredictability of Mobile's weather that gave me the hardest time. I have never watched the weather so much in my life! Sometimes, it was necessary to repack my art supplies quickly as gusts of wind and rain abruptly interrupted me. And then, the wetness was followed by a sudden furnace. Beyond the challenges that the Mobile weather presented, another difficulty was geography and the position of the wall on a sloping ground.

Despite these barriers, it was the support of the Africatown community with their helping hands and strong backs and their sincere investment in my being able to finish the mural that saved me precious time, found me the necessary art supplies, and motivated me to persevere through the discomfort of the wind, rain and the heat.

Right now, I can say gracefully, that I am proud to have had this very beautiful art adventure. I am especially proud that I have contributed in my own way to the vast enterprise of rehabilitation and the rebirth of Africatown. My mural will welcome people to the emergence of the future Africatown and link the African past to the Africatown present and future.

I create Art that makes sense; it is a principle that I also have applied over the last few years in my other art form of music. Just as I chose to weave history into the mural, I sing songs with historical themes in order to bring History to those who are not looking for it, but who will nevertheless retain aspect of it (a character, a date) as they recall the melody. Yes, we all need Art that makes sense!

©2023 Jeki Esso

MONUMENTAL ARCHITECTURE

Monumental architecture is found throughout Africa, in both ancient and modern buildings. The best-known examples are the pyramids, not only in Nubia (current Sudan) and in Egypt, but also in ancient Ghana, Mali and Niger. The Great Wall of Zimbabwe is another example of monumental construction, and we should also mention the Walls of Benin City in Nigeria and the castle of Gondar in Ethiopia.

On a smaller scale, in terms of housing, we need only look to the Musgum houses and the Bamileke temple-palaces in Cameroon, the small Tamberma and Tata castles (Togo and Republic of Benin), the Ndomo building in Mali, the Basotho houses in Lesotho, etc. These constructions were historically made of stone, clay, raw or terracotta or even wood.

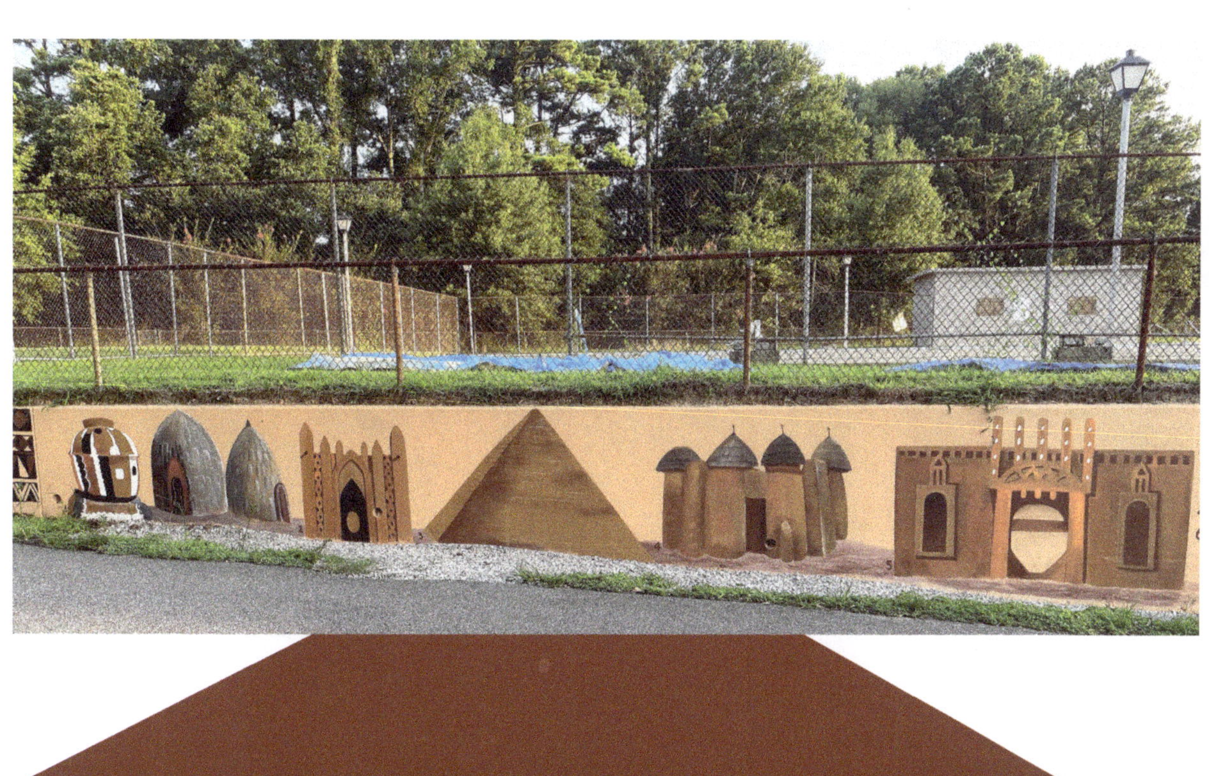

Kassena Mural Painting

The houses are traditionally painted by women, with natural pigments, plaster, kaolin, *néré*, (a local tree) laterite, pebbles, chalk, plant decoctions. In place of brushes, they use bird feathers to paint. The Kassena people are found in southern Burkina Faso and Ghana.

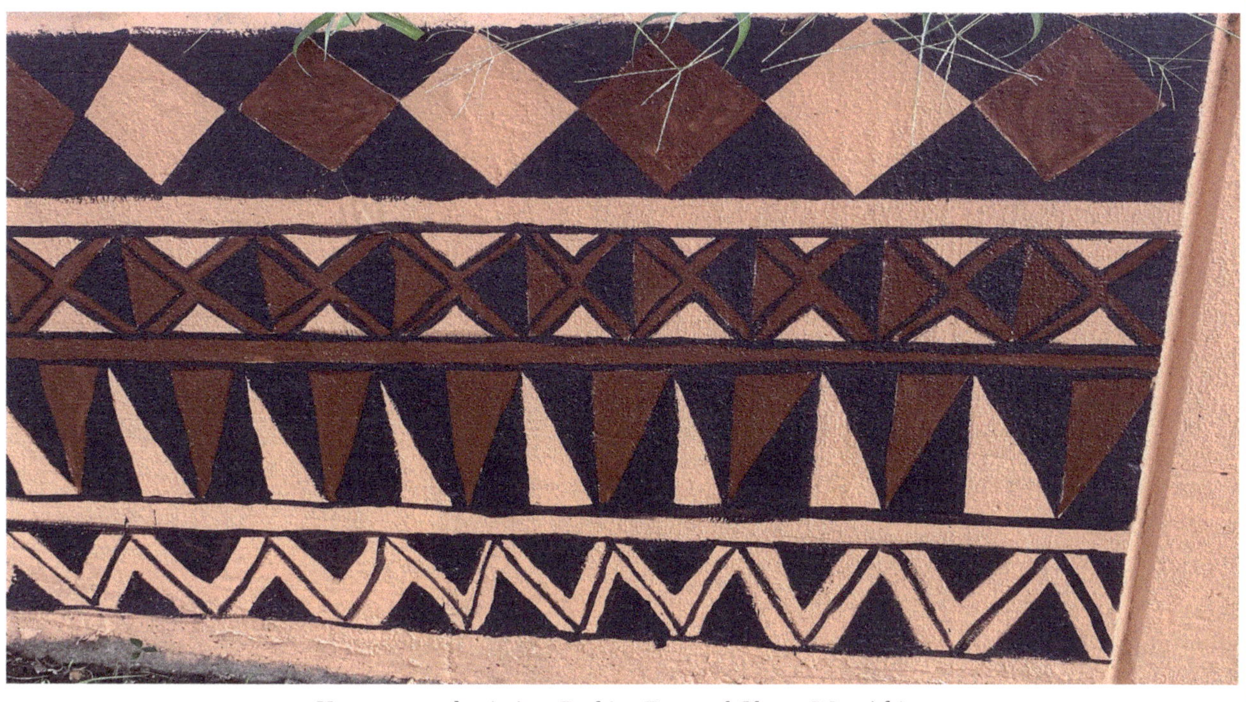

Kassena mural painting, Burkina Faso and Ghana, West Africa.

A Granary in a Musgum Village

Grain storage and *Musgum houses:* these dwellings are constructed with a mixture of earth, clay, manure and grass, and are built without foundations or reinforcements; they range in size up to 82 feet, and sometimes are 23 feet in diameter. The Musgum people are located in the North of Cameroon.

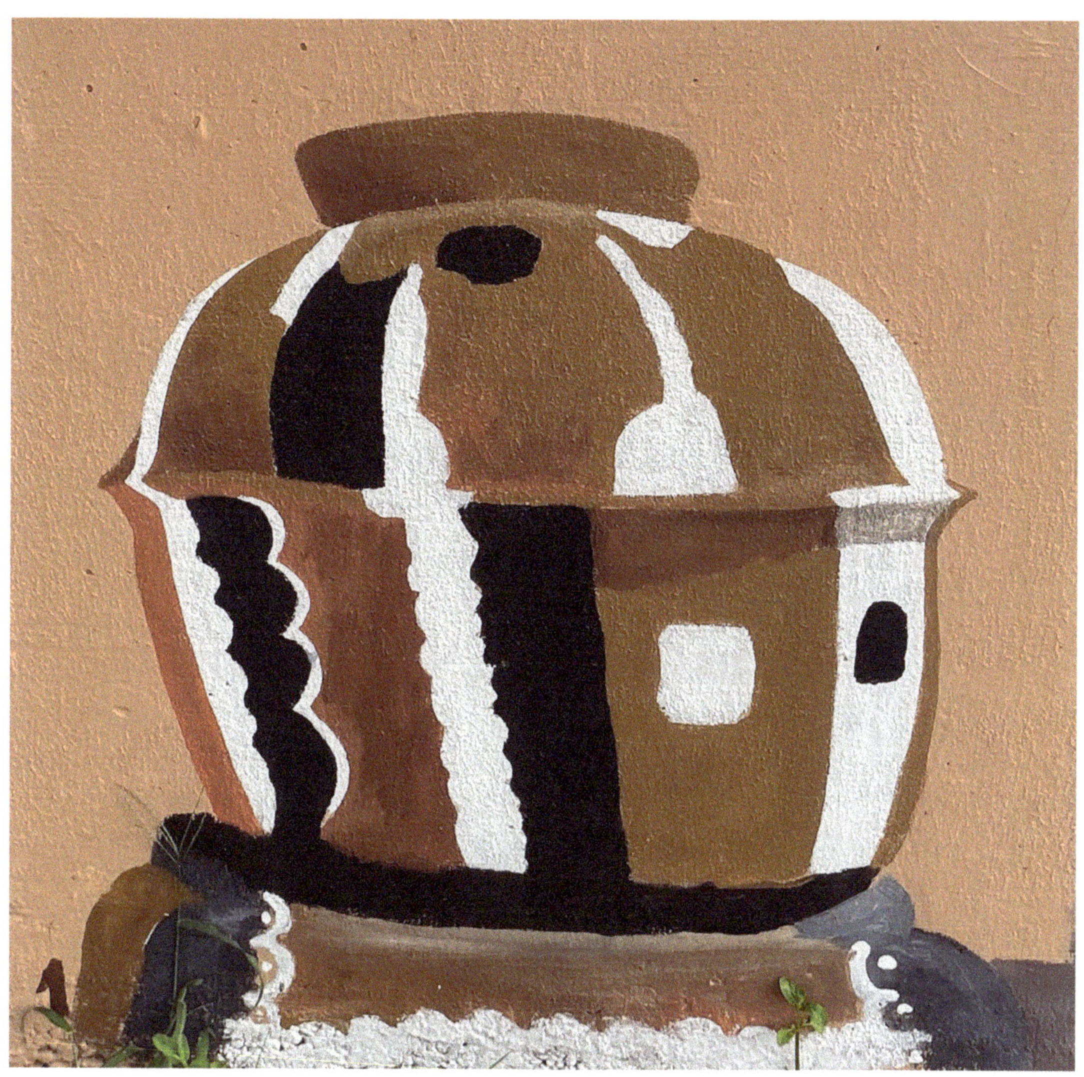

A Granary in a Musgum Village

Musgum Houses

Musgum houses: these dwellings are constructed with a mixture of earth, clay, manure and grass, and are built without foundations or reinforcements; they range in size up to 82 feet, and sometimes are 23 feet in diameter. The Musgum people are located in the North of Cameroon.

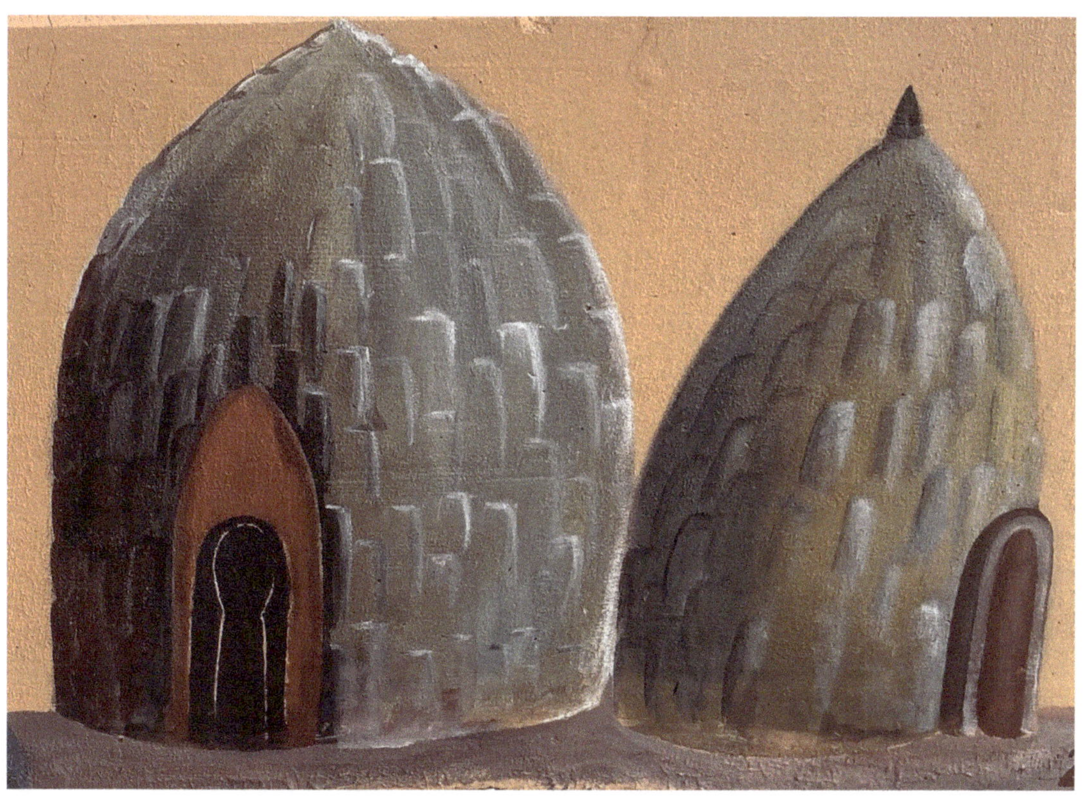

Musgum houses in Northern Cameroon.

Sudanese Sahelian West African Architecture

Past and Present

There are several examples of this clay and banco brick, also called Sudano-Sahelian, architecture in Mali, Niger, Nigeria, Burkina Faso, Benin, and Ghana.

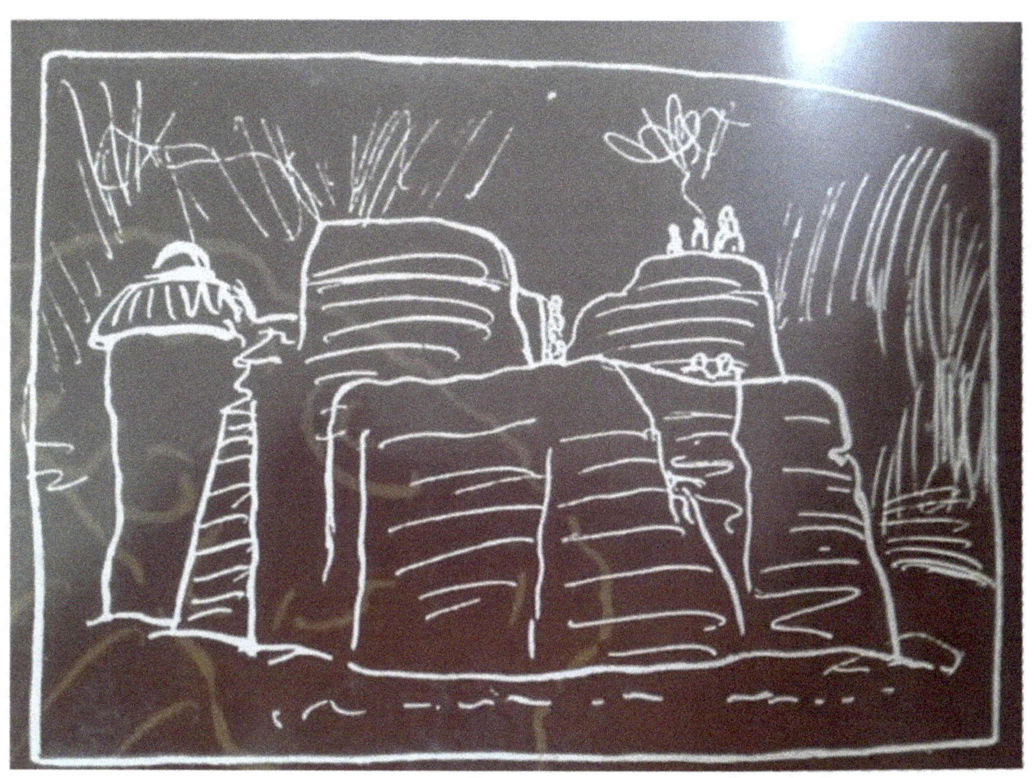

A fortified palace. Transkara, Togo. In *L'Art Nègre*, Vladimir Markov, preface from Dieudonné Gnammankou, Monde Global 2006, p42

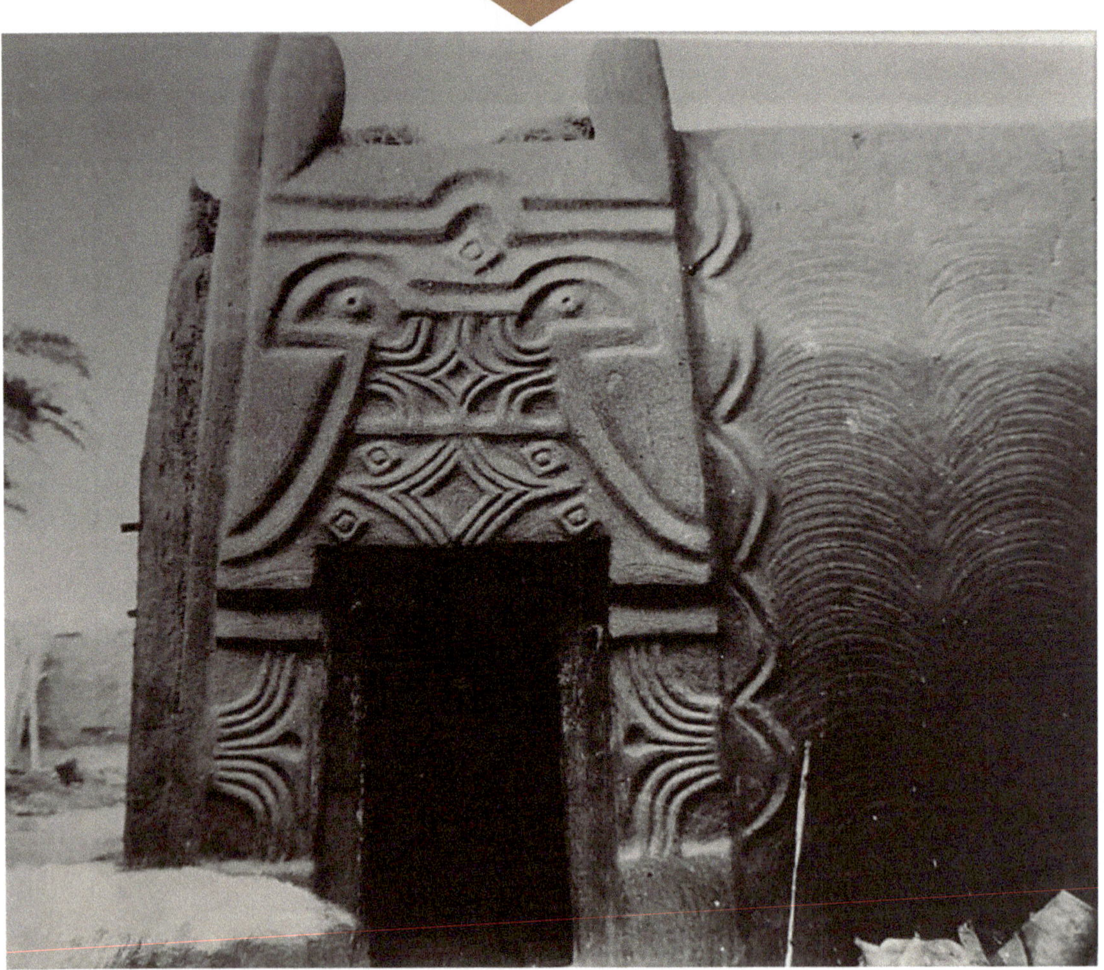

A Hausa house in Kano, Nigeria.

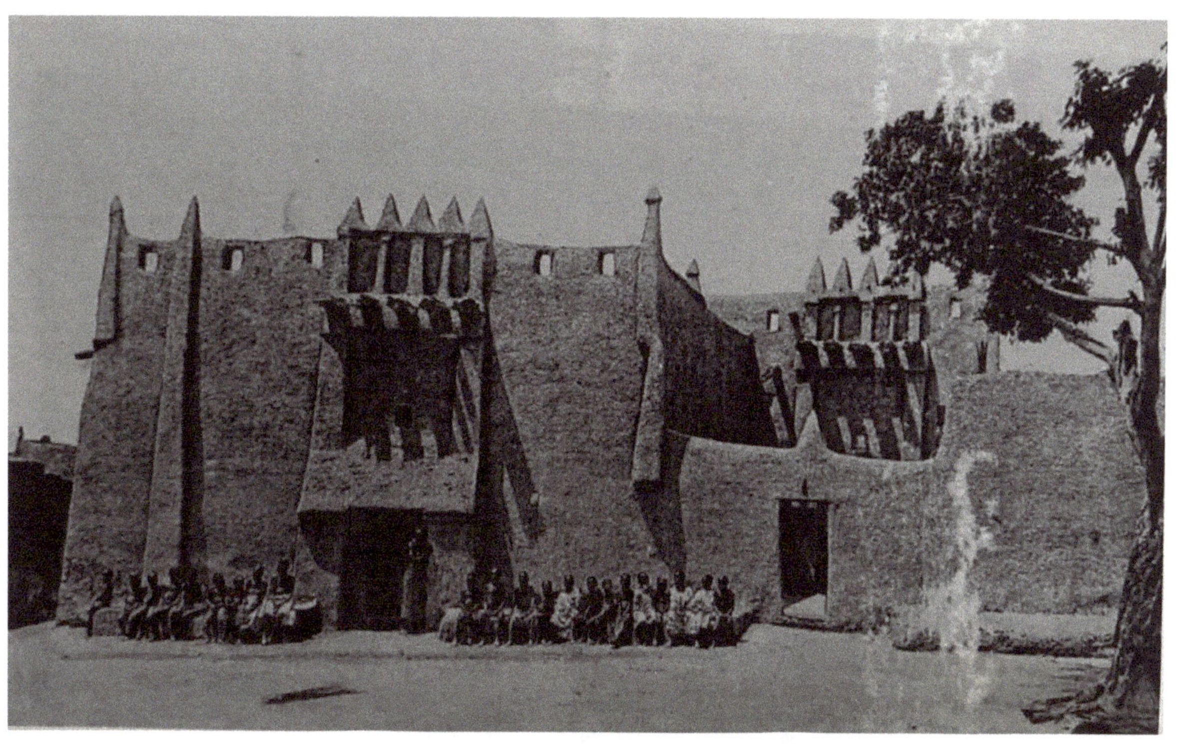

House of a dignitary. Djenné, Songhay. Mali.

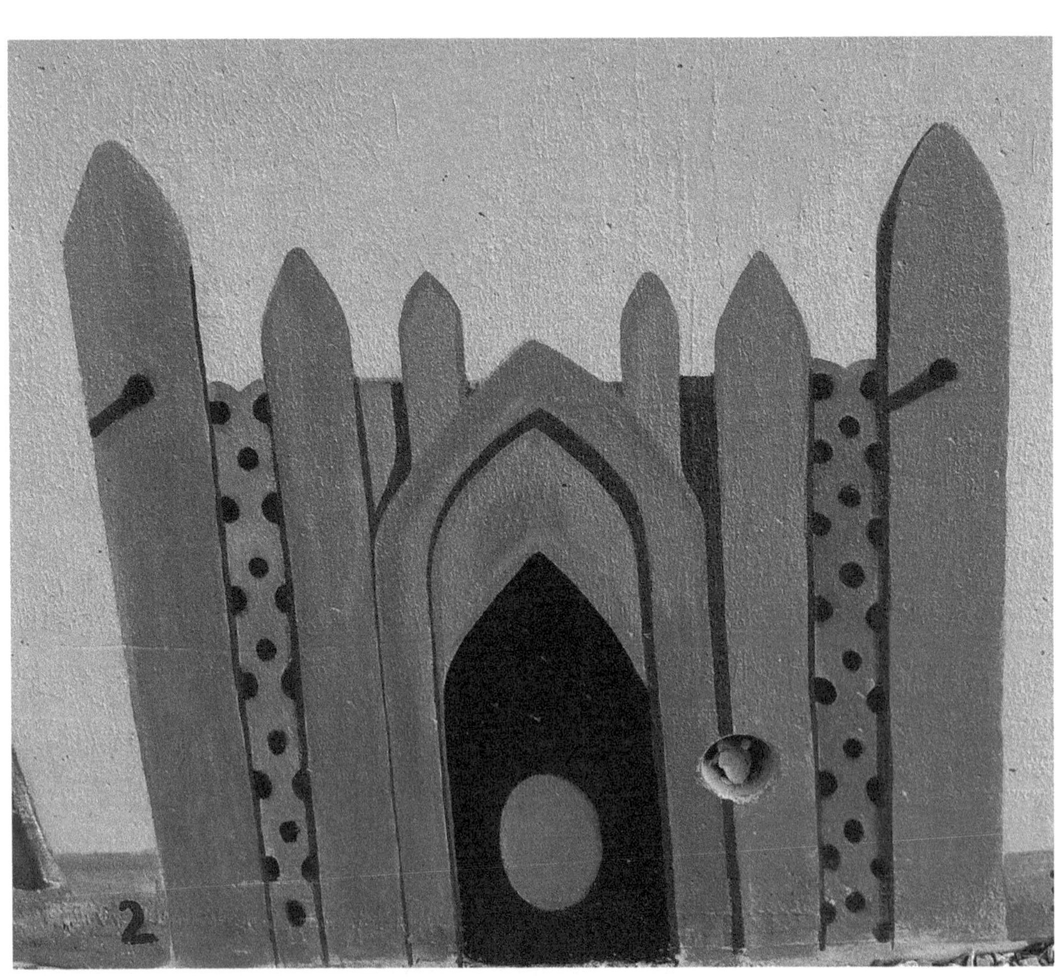

A public building. Segou, Mali.

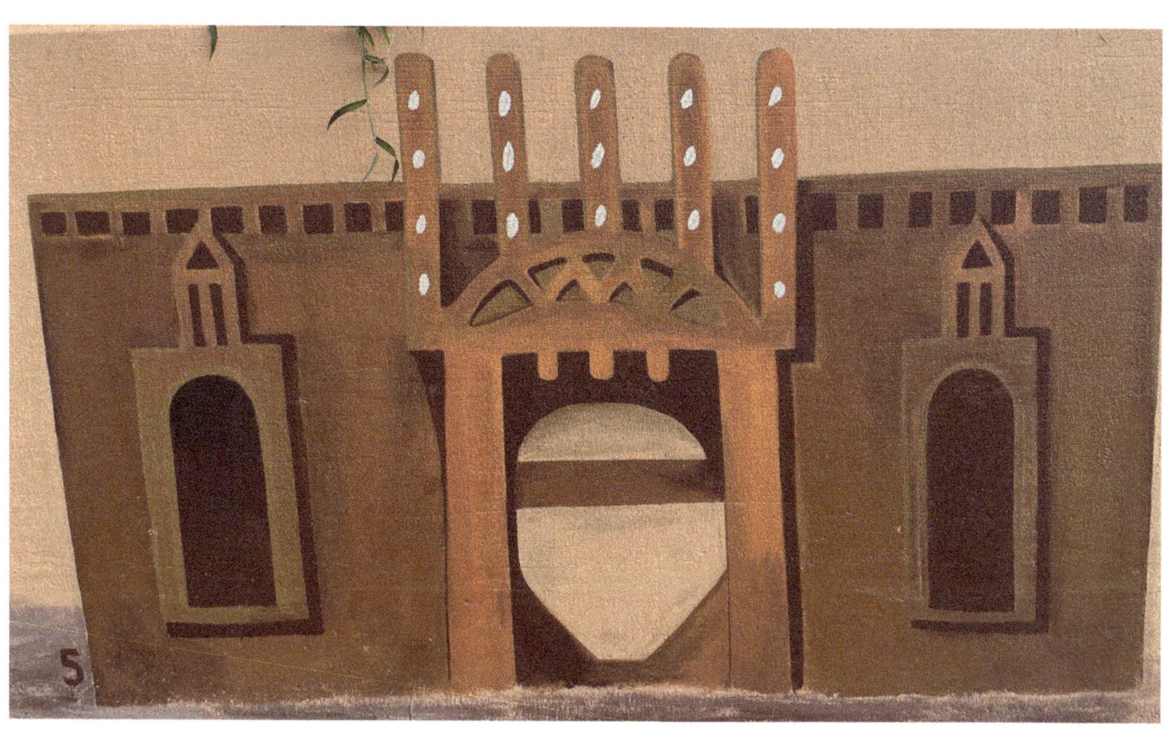

Modern building. The conservatory of traditional textile dyeing techniques. Segou, Mali.

An Egyptian pyramid

This monumental construction is undoubtedly a powerful emblem of Kemet or ancient Egypt. However, contrary to popular belief, the oldest example of this type of architecture are found in Sudan. Several peoples having migrated from Sudan to other regions of Africa; as a result, we find the miniaturized pyramidal shape in certain roofs of "huts."

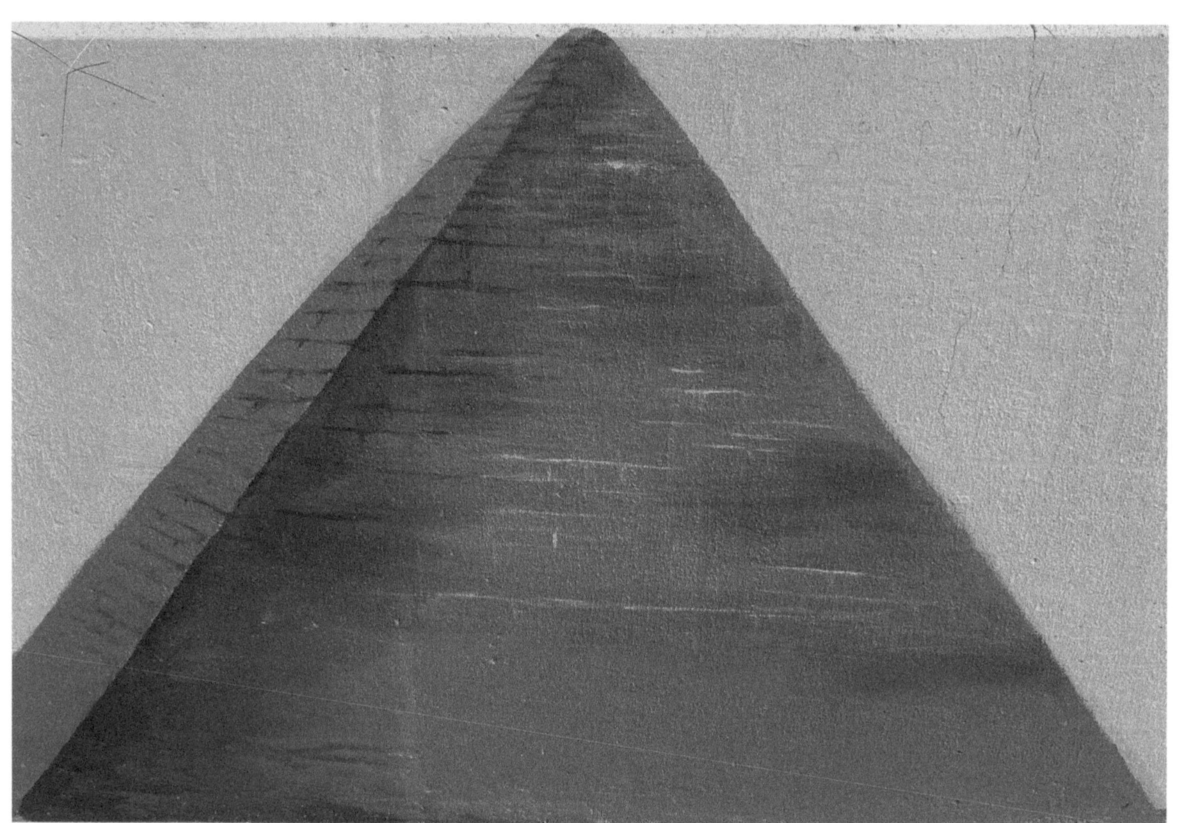

Ancient pyramid, Land of Kemi, Kemet, Egypt.

Batammariba Tata or Tamberma

These miniature castles are located in North Benin and Togo and are constructed out of raw earth and plants; the floor is made up of a mixture of wood, earth and leaves. They serve both as habitat and granary for the Berba, Natemba, Otammari, Waaba, Yende and Batammari peoples.

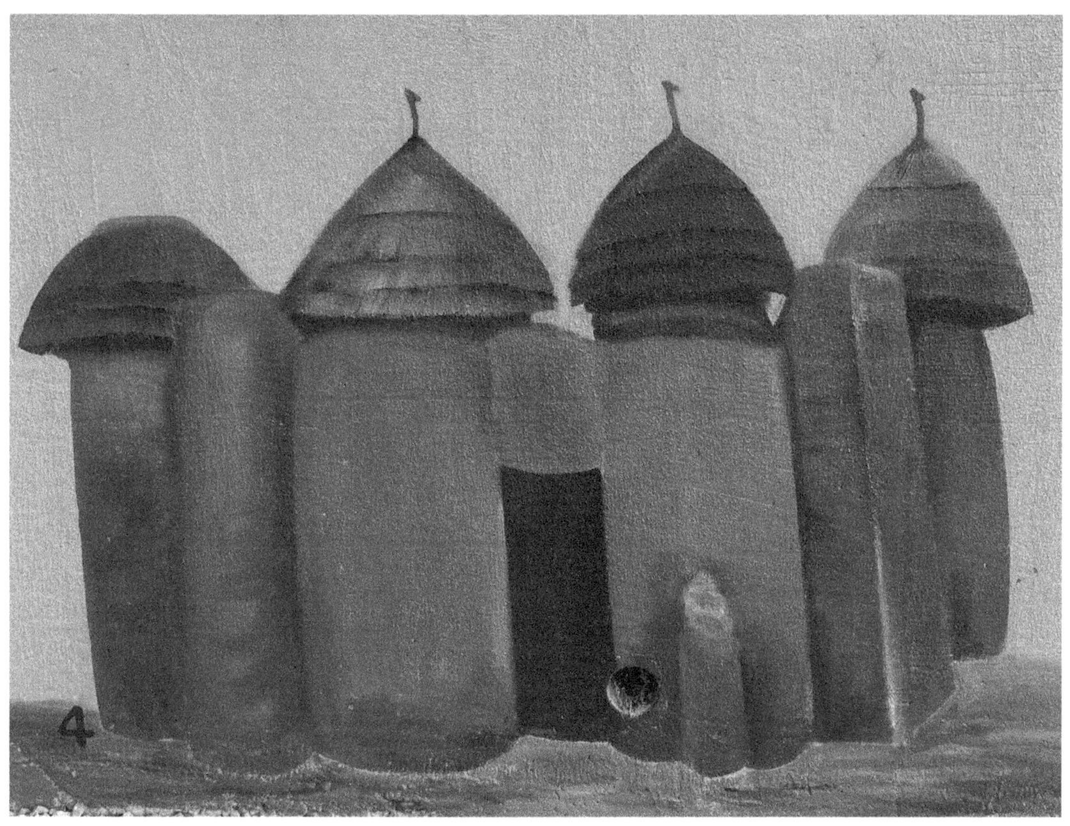

Batammariba Tata: A miniature castle in Benin.

Gondar Castle

This monumental construction is called Fasil Ghebi after the Ethiopian emperor Fasilides in the 17th century. Gondar was the center of the Ethiopian government until 1864. The fortified enclosure is made up of six main bodies of buildings surrounded by a 900 meter (0.559 mile) long rampart.

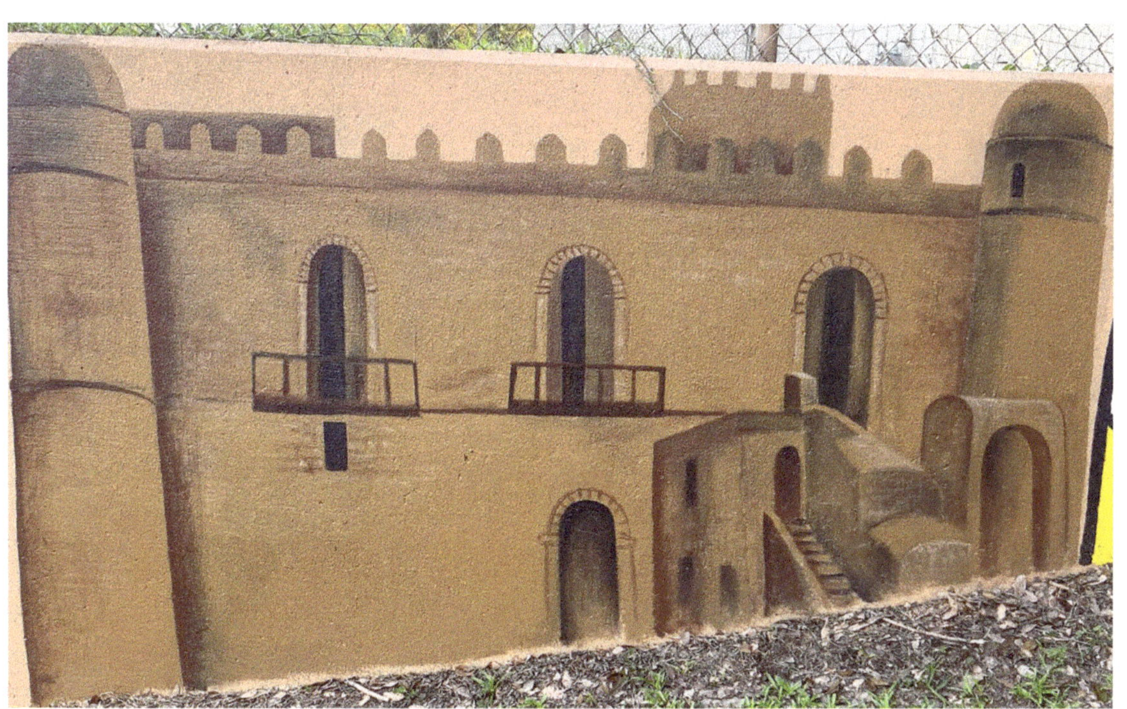

Gondar Castle, Ethiopia.

Ndebele Mural Painting

This structure is characterized by geometric patterns and vibrant colors. The Ndebele people live in South Africa and Zimbabwe, and the murals on the houses are made exclusively by women. Historically, these decorations symbolized cultural resistance and continuity in the face of the oppression of colonial Dutch settlers; unaware of the hidden messages, this colonial power considered this art to be innocent, which allowed it to continue. Some of these symbols allowed the Ndebele to communicate secretly. Today this art, which is transmitted from mother to daughter, expresses clan membership, identity, rites of passage, values, and feelings, and also can indicate social status.

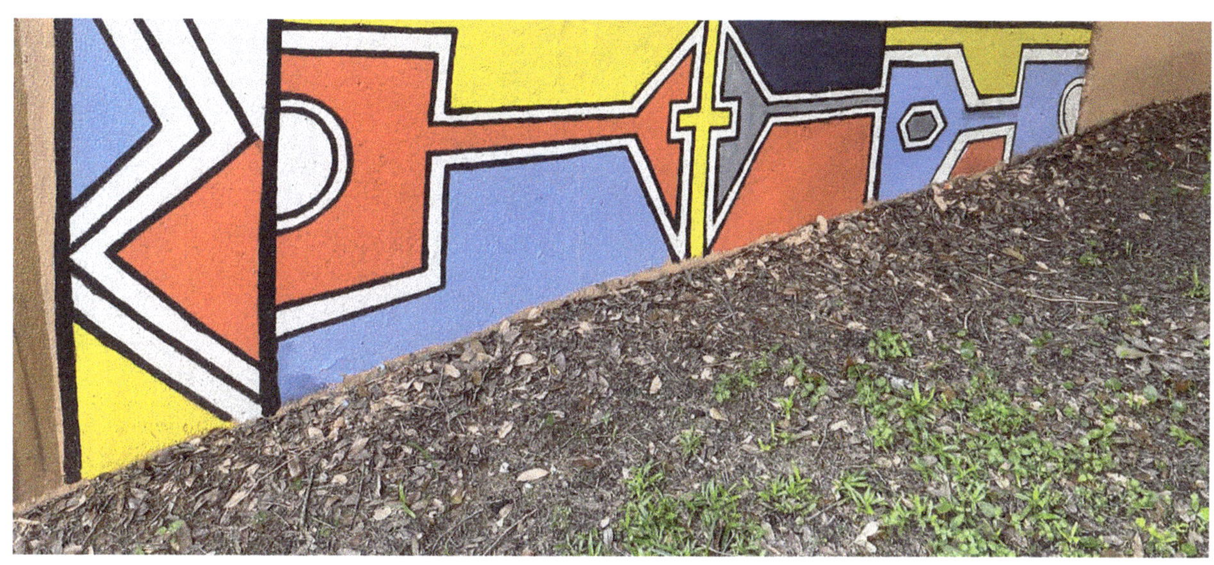

Ndebele Mural Painting, South Africa.

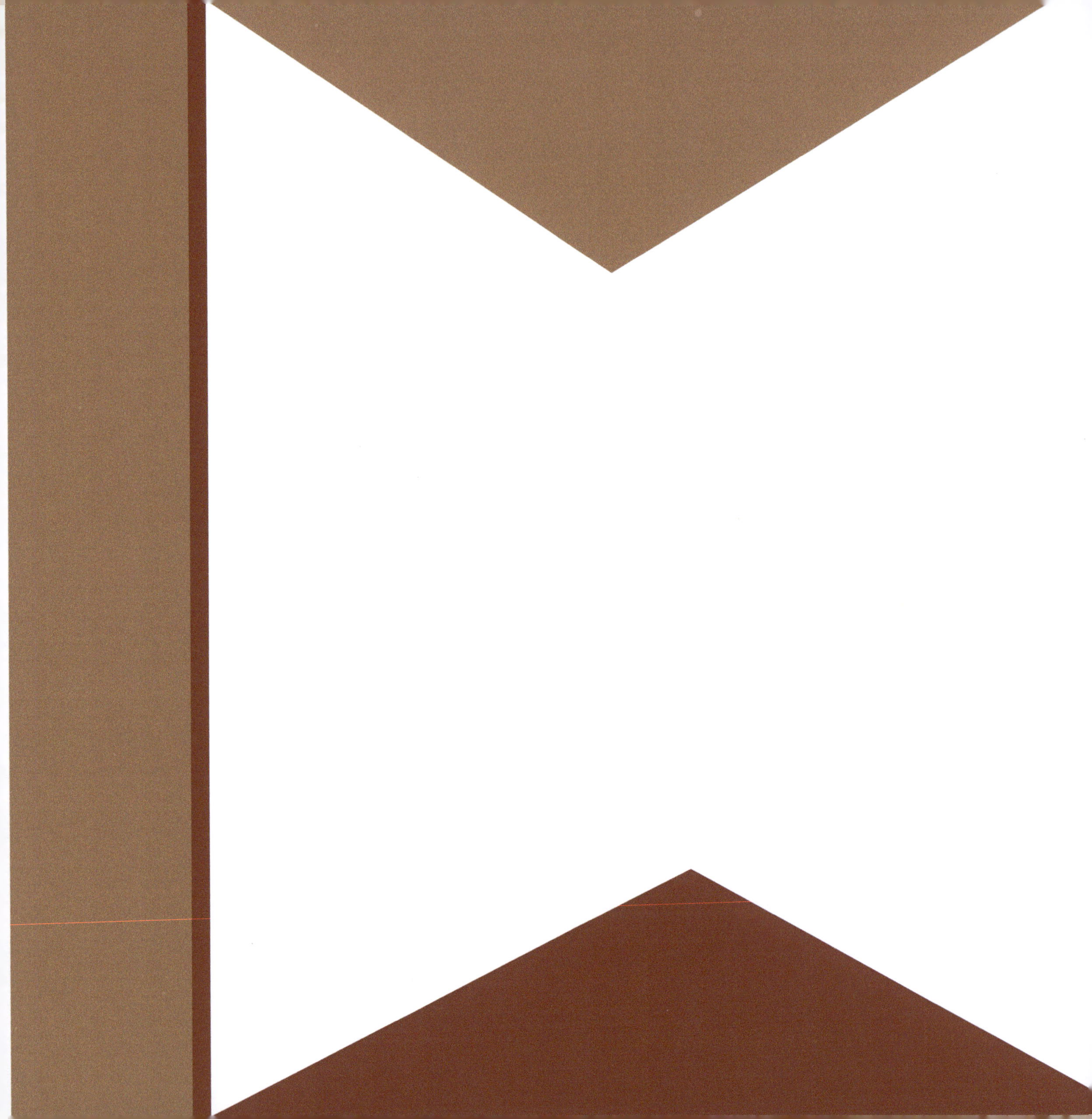

PHILOSOPHY : SYMBOLS AND CONCEPTS
PART I

Adinkra symbols are ideograms. They represent the values and thoughts of the Akan people who live in Ghana and the Ivory Coast. It is truly a form of writing. Below is a description of the meaning of each symbol. In Benin, the artistic and graphic traditions of bas-reliefs on the walls are still present.

Sankofa: Learning from the past. Adinkra, Ghana
Energy. Adinkra, Ghana
Beetle: Rebirth or Resurrection. Land of Kemi, Kemet, Ancient Egypt
 Dwennimen: Strength, Adinkra, Ghana
Dan (The Snake biting his tail): Abundance. Dahomay

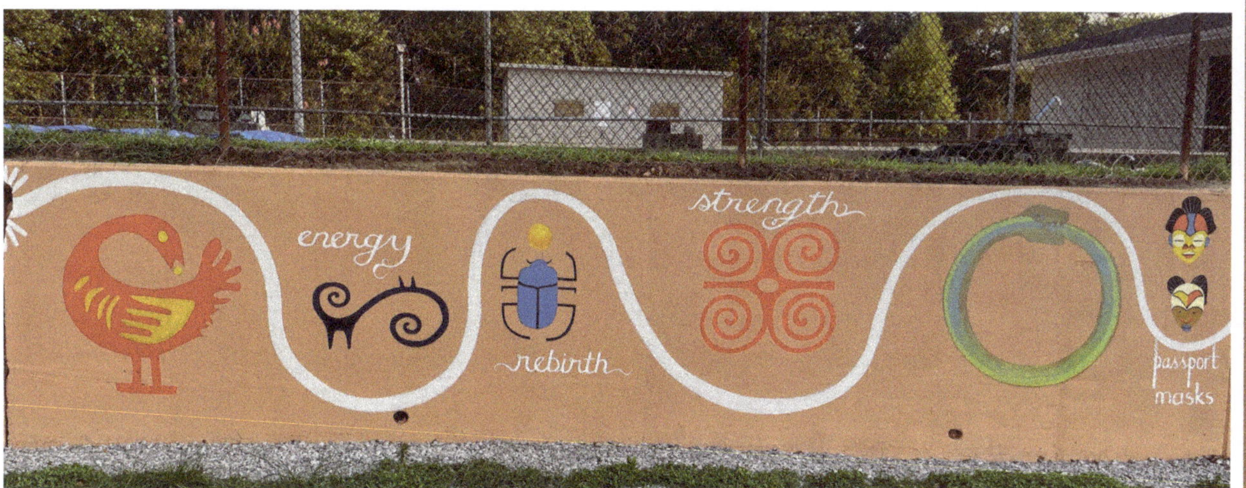

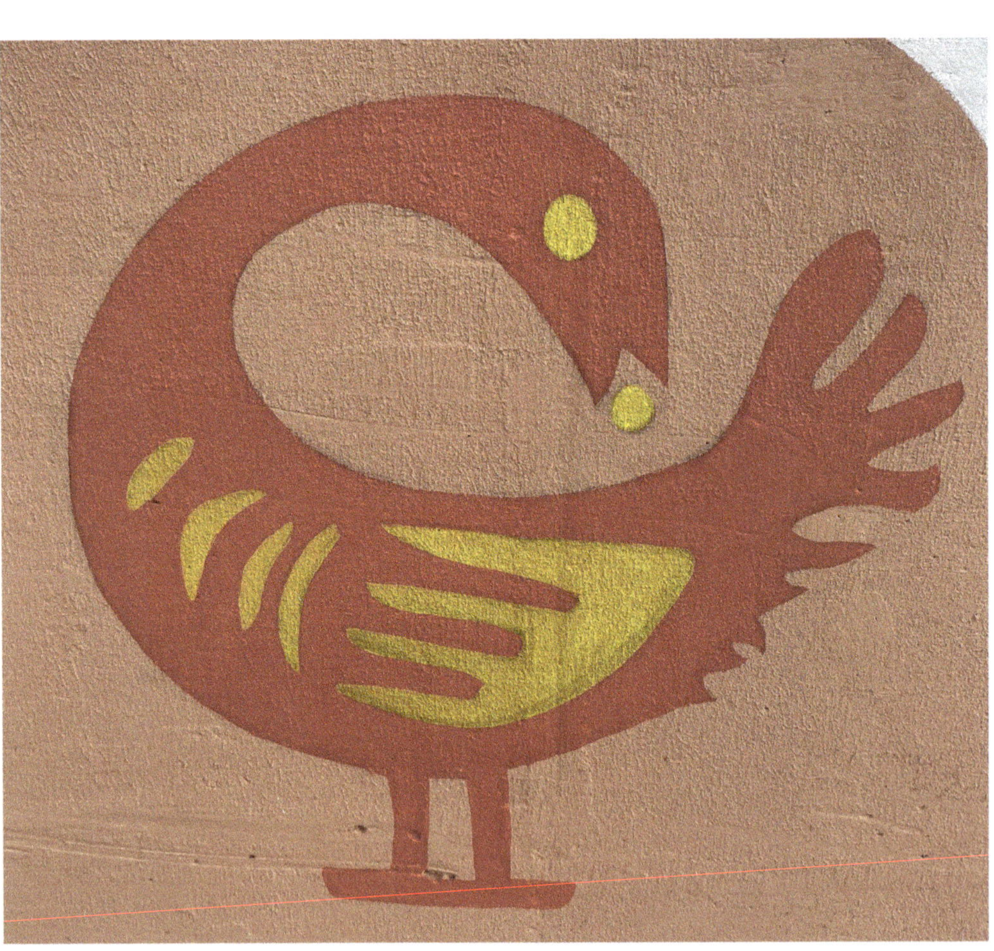

Sankofa: Learning from the past. Adinkra, Ghana.

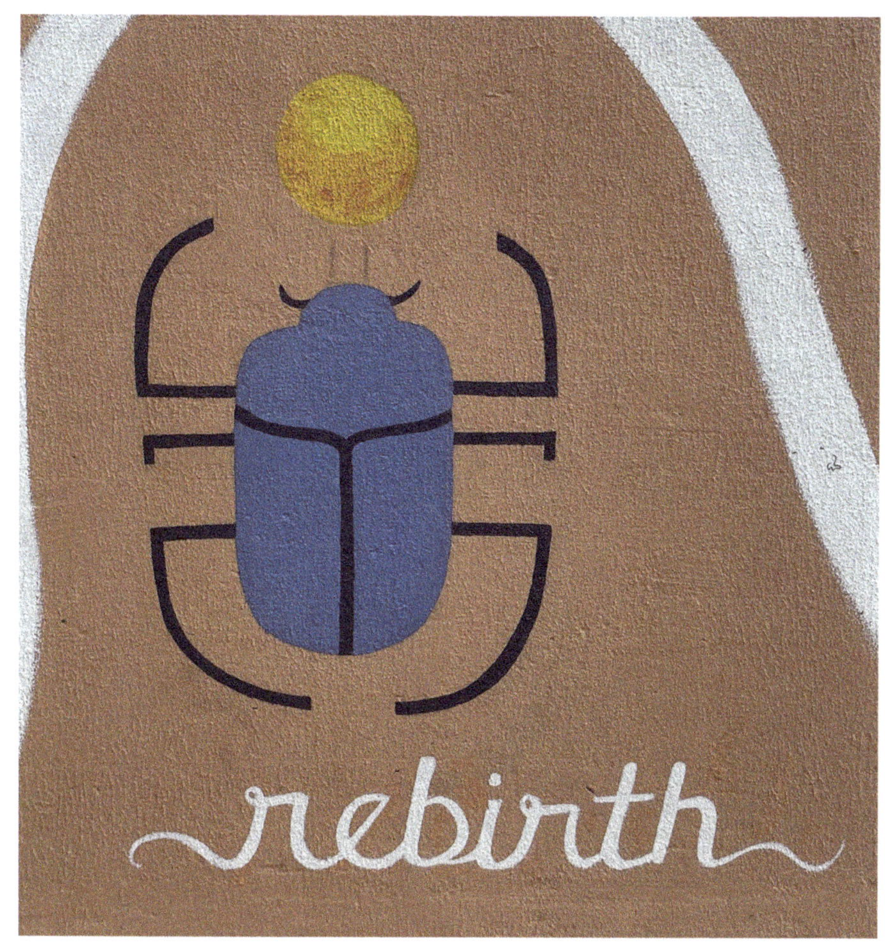

Beetle: Rebirth or Resurrection. Land of Kemi, Kemet, Ancient Egypt.

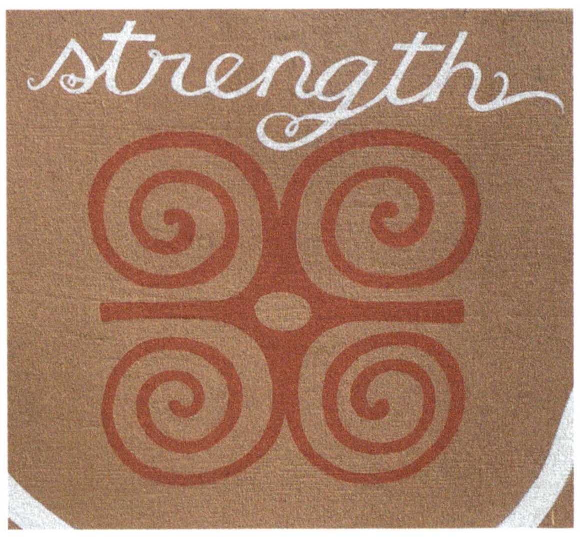

Dwennimen: strength, Adinkra, Ghana.

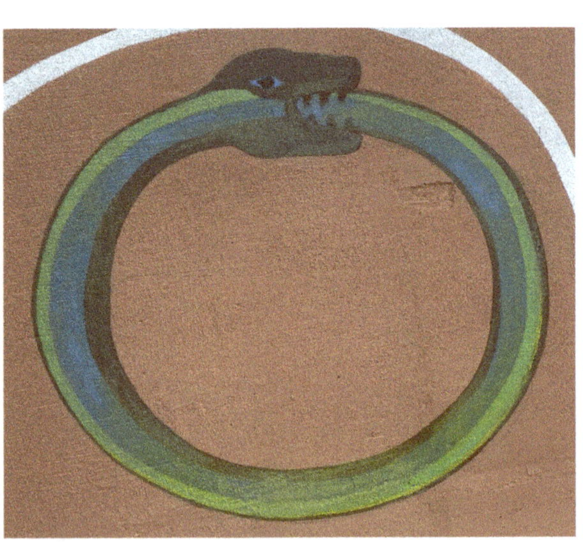

Dan: abundance, Dahomey.

SCIENCE

Africa is the cradle of modern science. The bones of *Lebombo* (35,000 years old, Eswatini) and *Ishango* (25,000 years old, Congo), the two oldest calculators in the world, prove that mathematics was practiced in Africa from time immemorial. The ocher stone of *Blombos* (80,000 years old, South Africa) has graphic lines in the form of regular triangles and reveal a triangulation system identical to that used today by GPS.

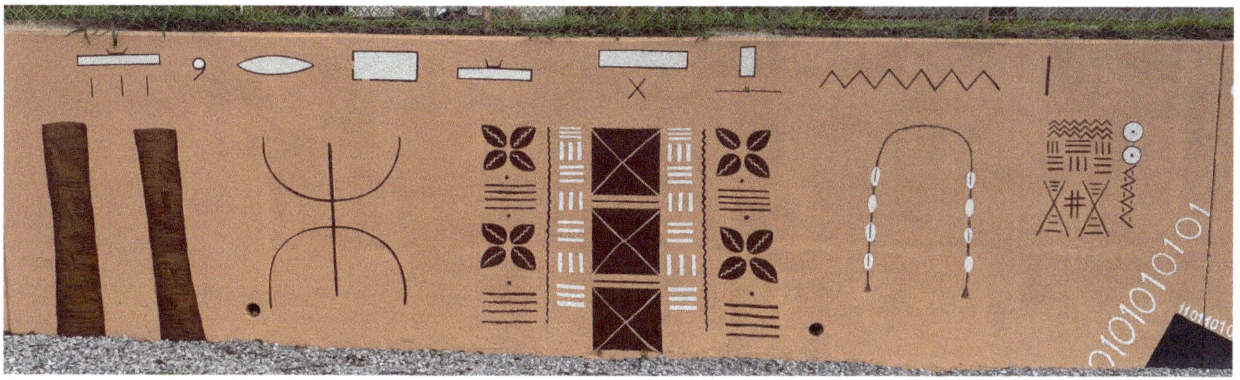

The wall of sciences.

Ancient mathematics

This is an excerpt from an ancient Egyptian mathematical formula dating back approximately 2000 years BC (Papyrus of Ahmes or Rhind Papyrus).

Full text of Moscow Papyrus Issue No. 10, after T. E. Peet. (T.E. Peet: 'A problem in Egyptian geometry', in J.E.A., tome 17, 1931, p. 100-106, pl. XVIII.)

Source: "Cheikh Anta Diop, Africa's contribution to the exact sciences", in ANKH n 6/7, 1997-1998, p 181.

Translation of the text of problem N 10
1. Method for calculating [the area] of a half-sphere
2. We tell you, a half-sphere (with an opening)
3. d of 4 1/2 (in diameter) oh

4. Can you tell me its area?
5. You calculate 1/9 of 9 because a half-sphere
6. Is half an egg. The result is 1.
7. Calculate the remainder, i.e. 8
8. Calculate 1/9 of 8
9. The result is $\frac{2}{3} + \frac{1}{6} + \frac{1}{18}$
10. Calculate the remainder of 8
11. After subtracting $\frac{2}{3} + \frac{1}{6} + \frac{1}{18}$ the result is $7 + 1/9$
12. Multiply 7 1/9 by 4 1/2
13. The result is 32, oh that's his area
14. You calculated it correctly.

In Cheikh Anta Diop, "contributions africaines aux sciences exactes", in ANKH n° 6, 1997-1998, p. 182

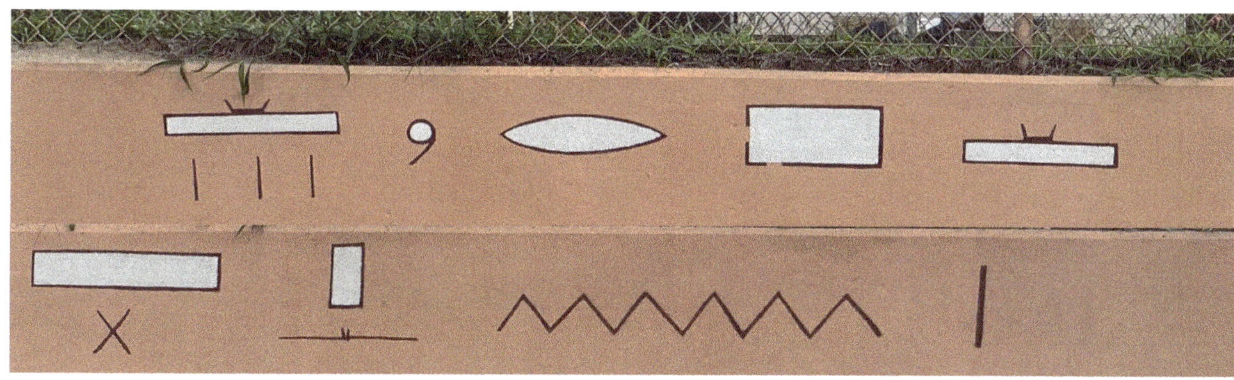

Problem in pyramid mathematics from the Ahmes papyrus (bought by Rhind). In Blacks in Science ancient and modern, Edited by Ivan van Sertima, Transaction Publishers, p 74.

Problem in pyramid mathemathics from the Ahmes papyrus -1650 BC, copied from a more ancient papyrus, 1900 BC under the reign of Amenemhat III (bought by Rhind in 1858). Preserved in the British Museum 110057 and 10058.

The Ishango bone

"A sophisticated calculator"..CNN
"A mathematical treasure". MAA
"The oldest evidence of the practice of mathematics in world history". Ankh, 12/13, 2003-2004.

This is a petrified bone adorned with a quartz crystal at the end and streaked with a series of notches. It measures about 3.9 inches long, and is in a museum in Belgium.

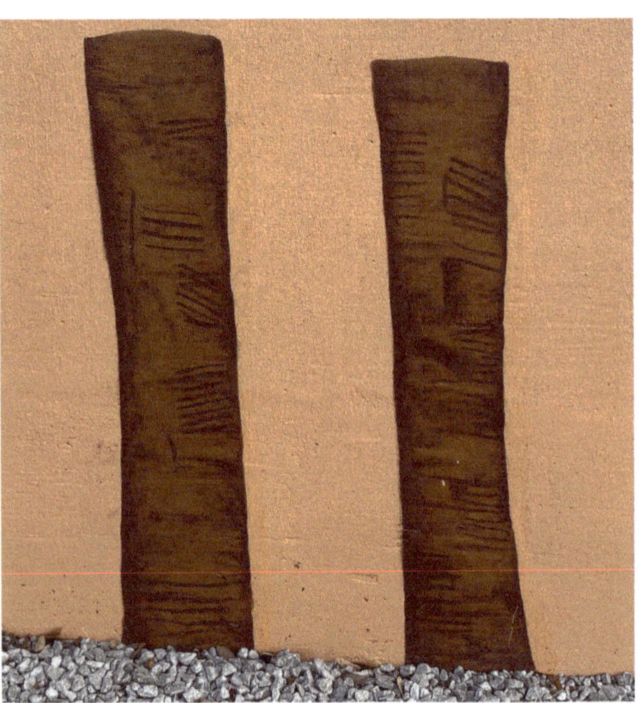

The Ishango bone.

Amazigh (the Berber) symbol of resistance : represents a free man

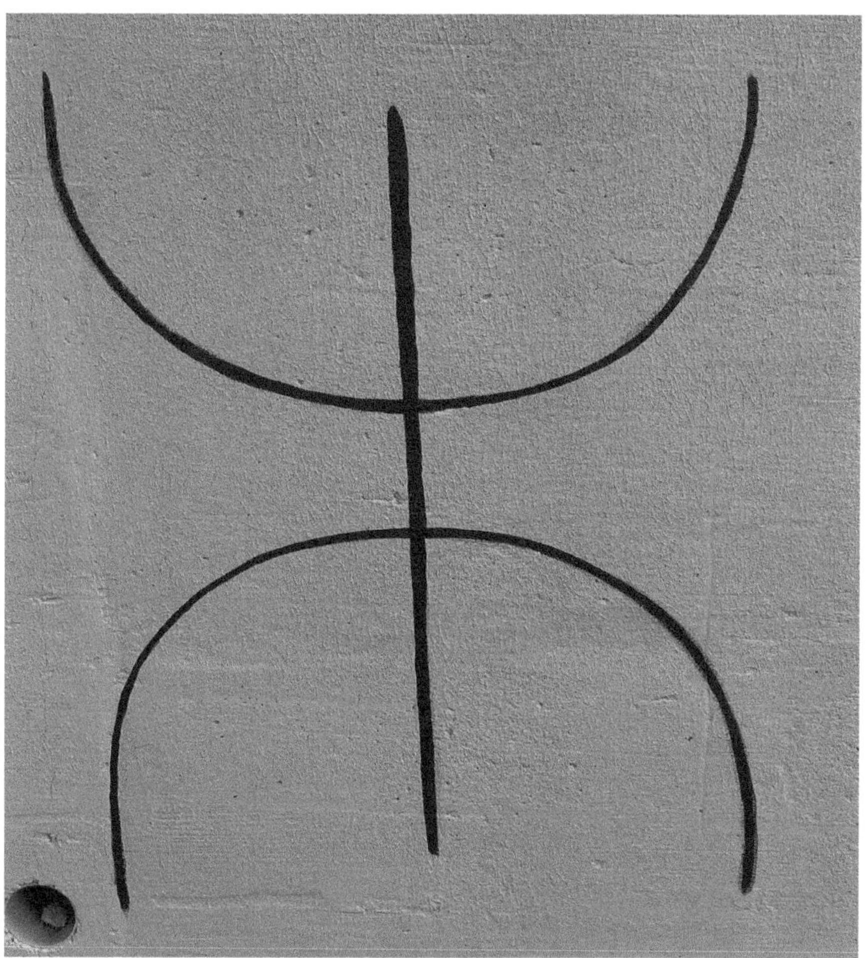

Berber writing system is called *Tifinagh*. This is the letter Z.

Fractals

In nature, certain objects repeat themselves regularly such as branches, leaves, blood vessels, or wings of certain insects; these are called a fractal or a self-repeating pattern. Fractals can be found everywhere: in nature (like tree branches), in math (like triangles), in computers (as mathematical formulas), in cloud formations, as well as in geography, rivers, and terrain (https://iternal.us/what-is-a-fractal/). Fractals are repeated patterns that go on forever. Fractals can be found in African braiding patterns and the prints of African fabrics.

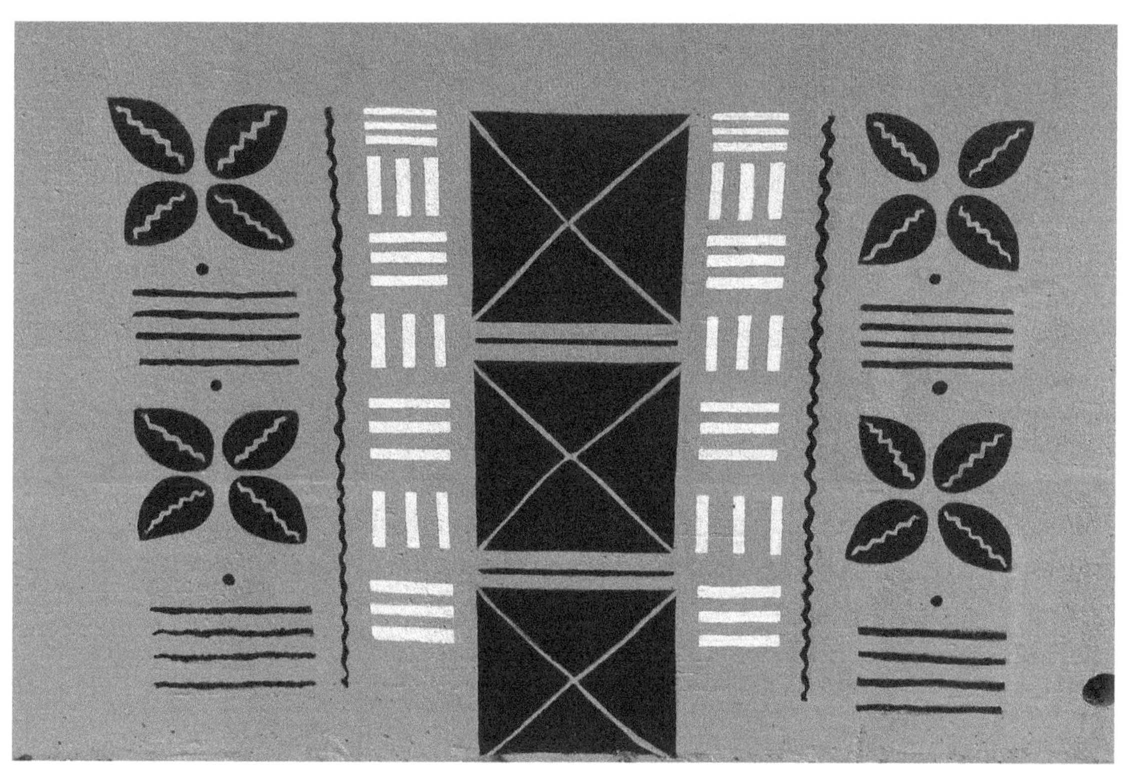

Example of fractals.

Okpele : Rosary of Ifa/fa/Afa

This object is called Okpele in Yoruba and is a symbol of divine knowledge; it is the ancestor of the octet (a group of eight). The Okpele dates back to 4000 years BC and is made up of 8 half-shells - a hollow side and a curved one; each shell has two faces, which makes it a binary element. While binary logic was theorized in the mid-19th century, and computing arrived nearly a century later, Africa was using a binary system centuries before its discovery by Europeans.

Source : LPP, Gratien Ahouanmenou.

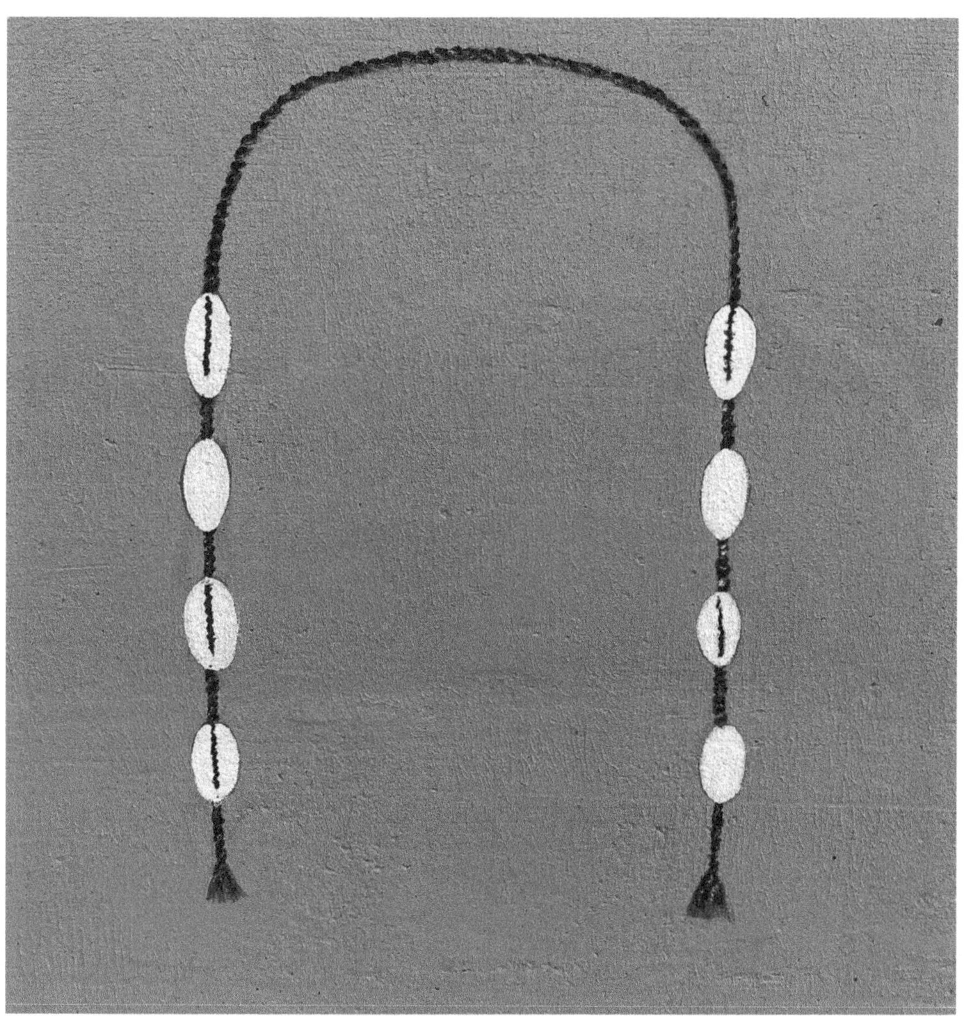

Okpele of ifa/Fa/Afa, Nigeria, Benin, Togo.

Dogon Formula

The Dogon people are found in Mali and have a rich culture and social heritage that included knowledge of the cosmos. The people of Mali are a scientific people and recognized today as astronomers without every using a telescope. They believe themselves to be descended from Ancient Egypt. They built ancient astronomical sites dedicated to the observation of Sirius and other "invisible stars" that modern science only confirmed existed in 1995 through the use of strong telescopes.

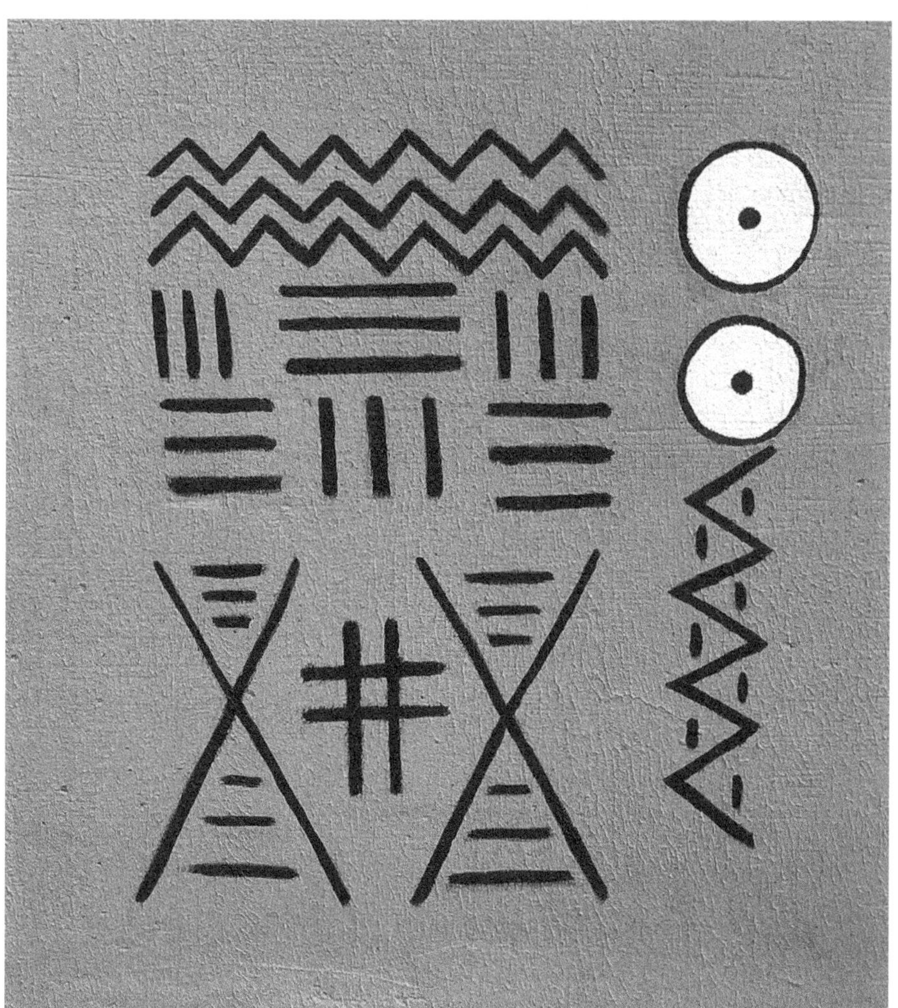

A Dogon formula.

Music

Traditional African Instruments: Music crossed the ocean with the Africans who arrived in the Americas and began to create their own instruments like the banjo, drums, and locally-made musical instruments from boxes and everyday objects like the washboard, while adapting European instruments to African-derived beats and rhythms. Everyone knows the huge impact African Americans have had on world music.

"Generally speaking, it is interesting to note that Africa has created an elaborate musical language. The Germans had great difficulty in conquering Cameroon because the villages warned each other to the sound of the drums of the actions and movements of the enemy. In some villages, at nightfall, when the time is quiet and calm, the drums exchange the news of the day."

In *L'Art negre*, Vladimir Markov, Monde Global 2006, p 57.

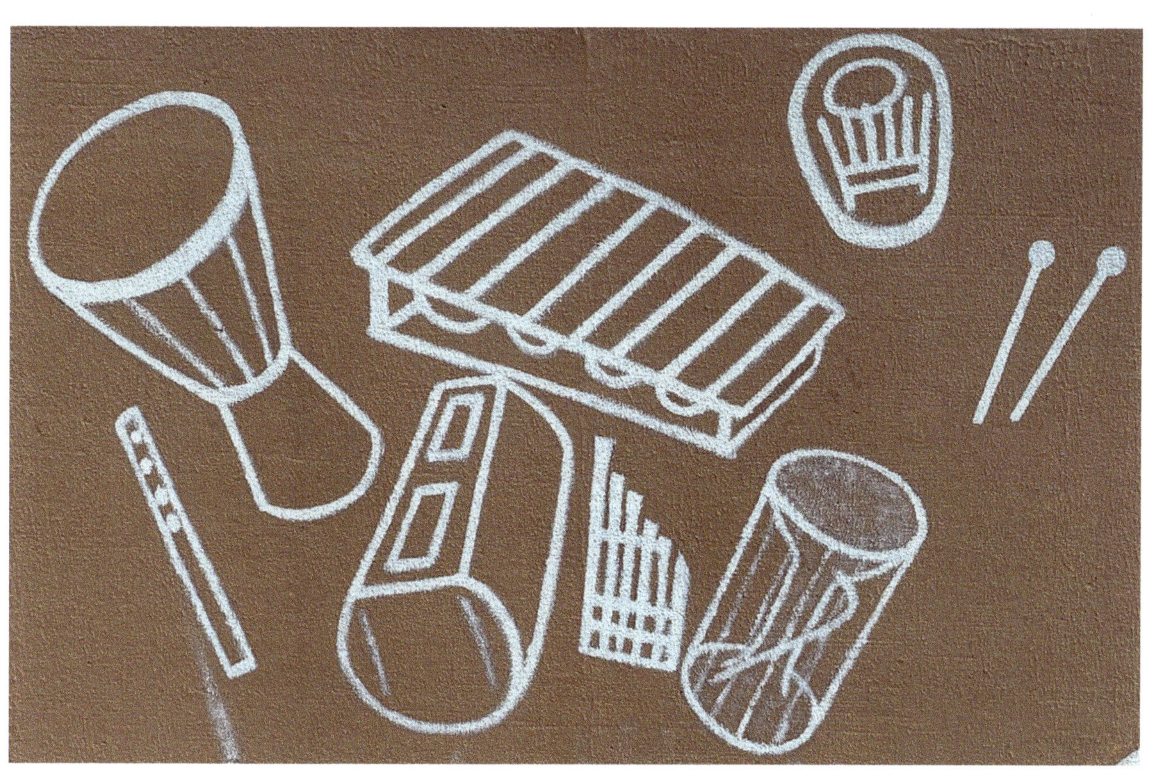

Some African tradional instruments.

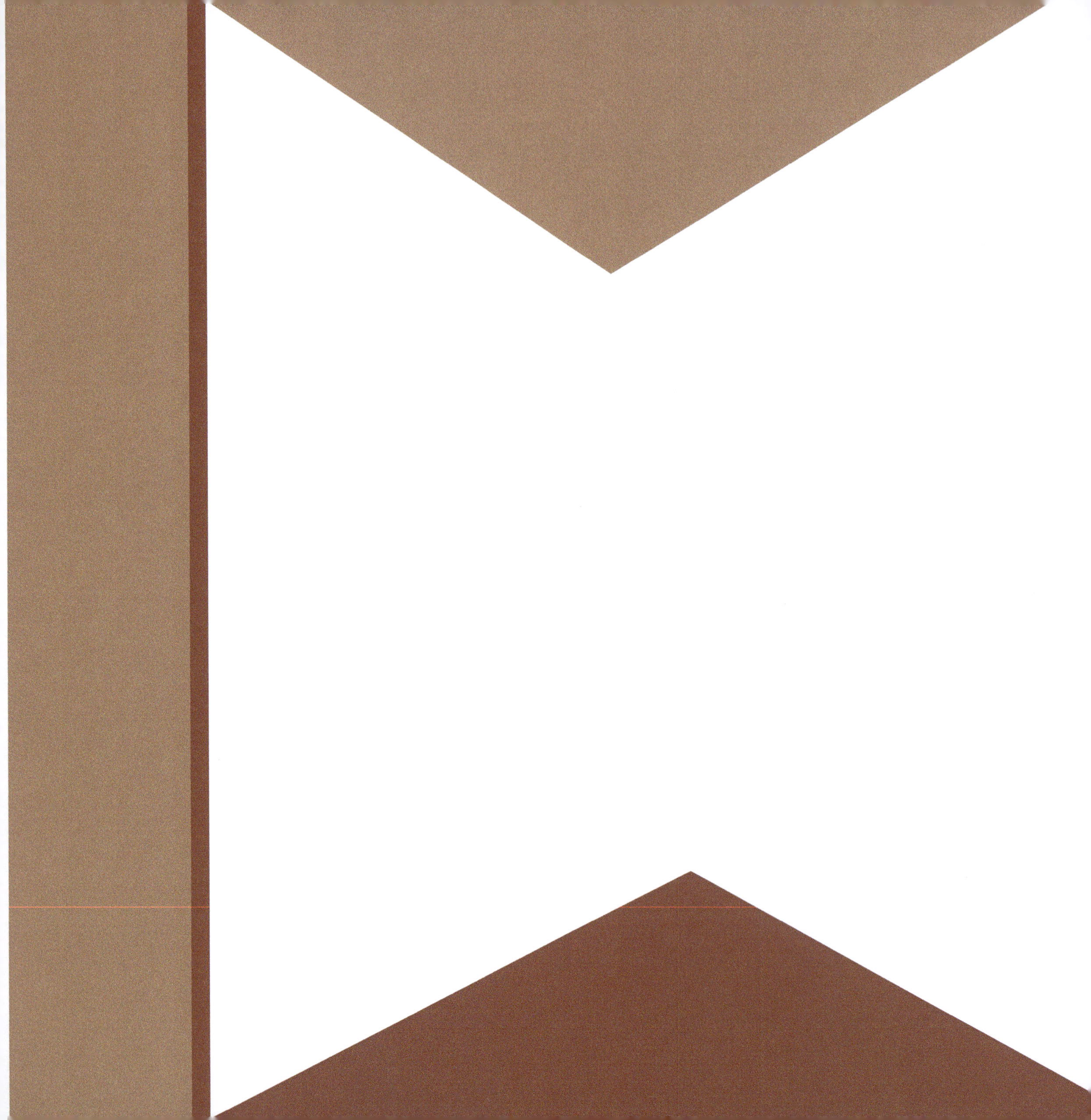

SYMBOLS AND CONCEPTS

PART II

Omotunde has several meanings: finding your way home; finding yourself and building a bridge between two continents; and rising from the ashes: unity, reconnection, rebirth. Inclusion of these three elements is intended to symbolize strengthening Africatown.

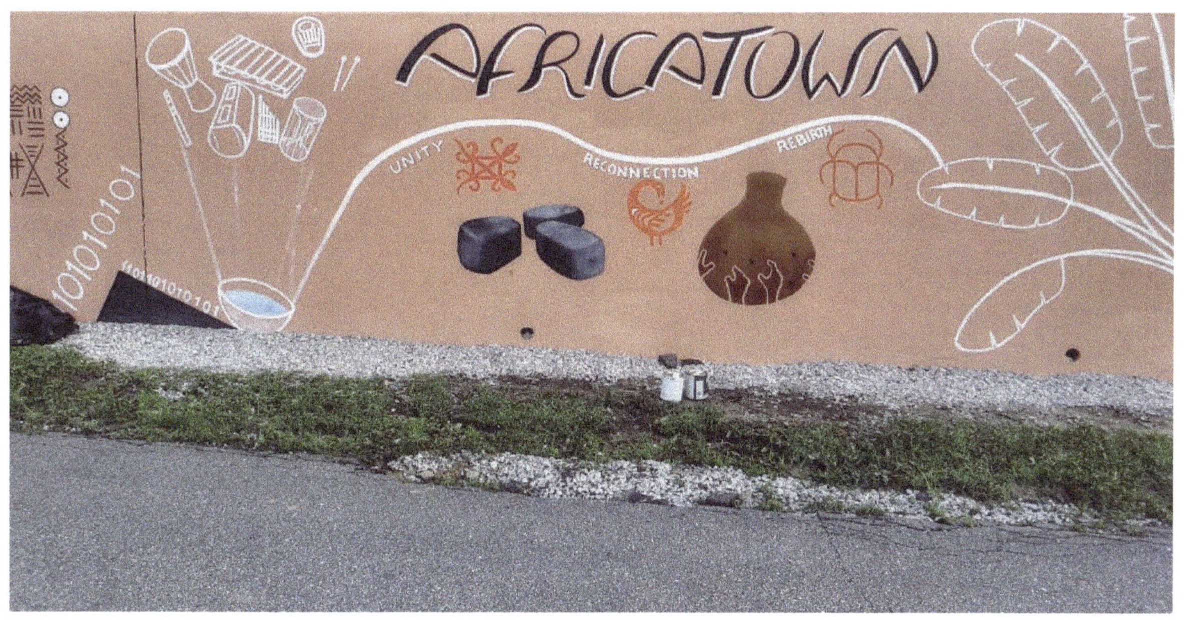

Calabash of water

Symbol of hospitality and peace

- The Calabash of water is a symbol of hospitality and peace.
- The three stones represent focus, stability and balance.
- The holed jar, sealed by several fingers, is a symbol of unity in Benin, because it is together that we will prevent the water from flowing out of the holes. This jar is meant to represent Africatown, the holes symbolize the problems of the community, and the fingers are the local people coming together to solve these problems.

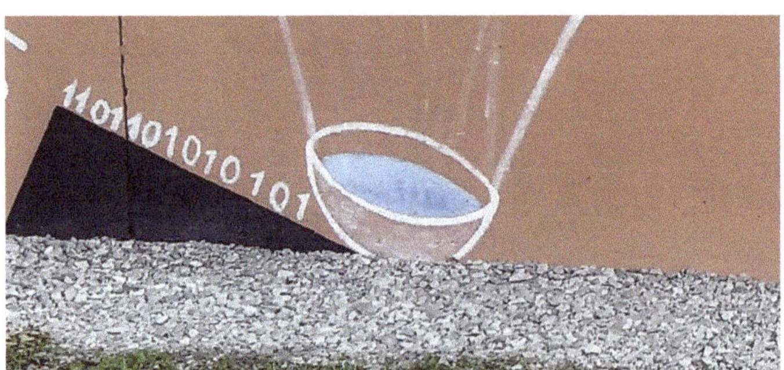
Calabash of Water.

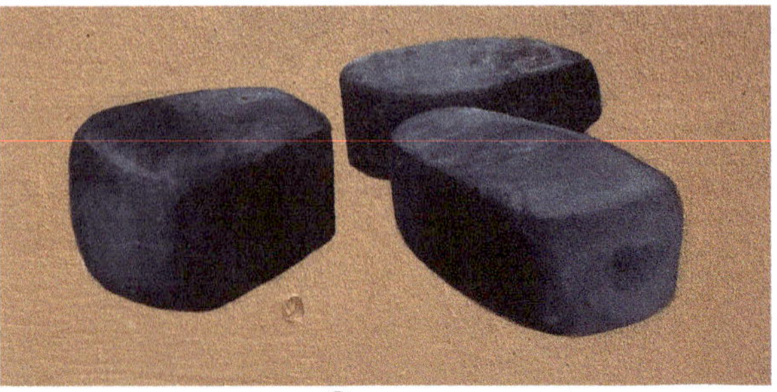
Stones

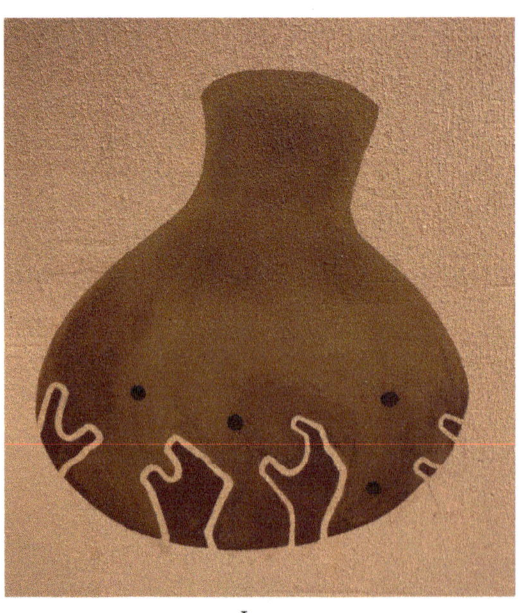
Jar

The double adinkra crocodile represents unity.

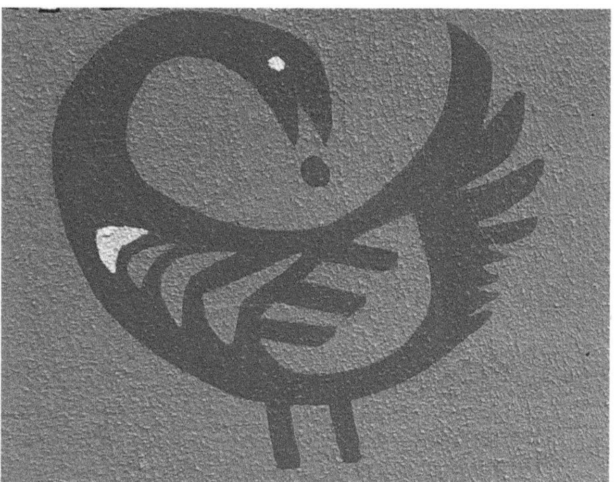

Sankofa means reconnection.

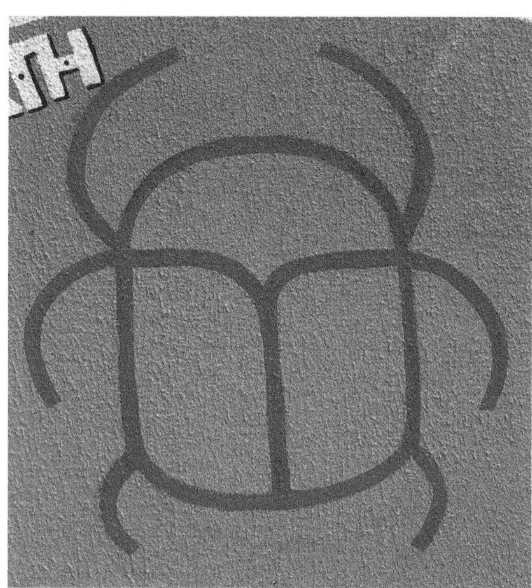

The beetle represents rebirth in the Land of Kemi, Kemet, Ancient Egypt..

Banana Tree

The banana tree is a symbol of the continuity of the works of our ancestors. Therefore, it is not surprising that these plants flourish throughout Africatown.

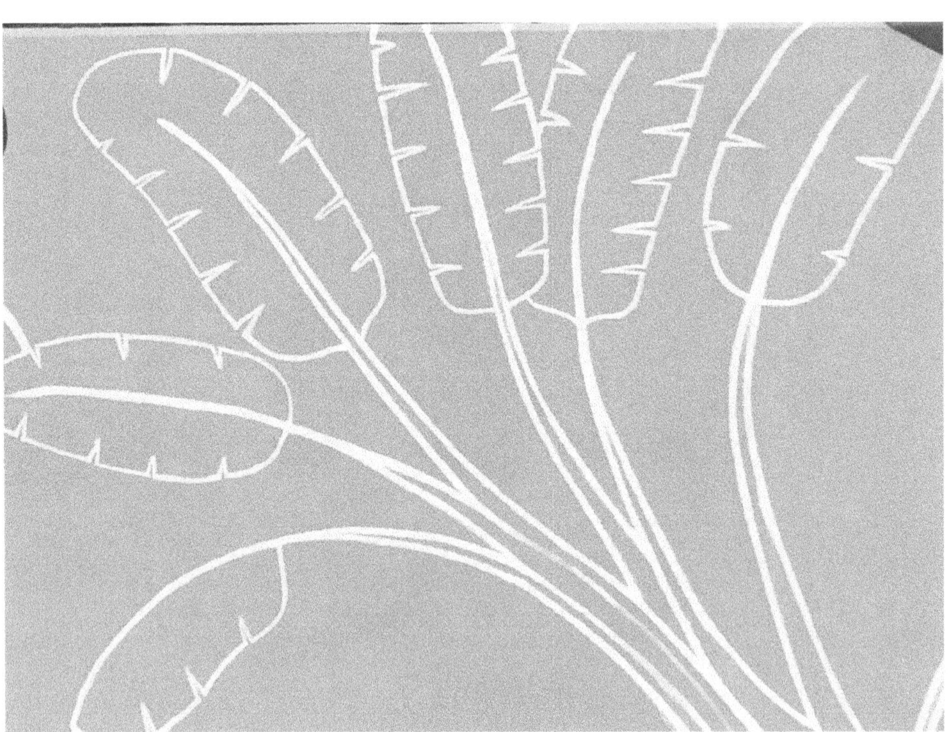

banana trees-mural.

Gye Nyamien

The *Gye Nyamien* is an adinkra symbol (Ghana) it means God is above everything.

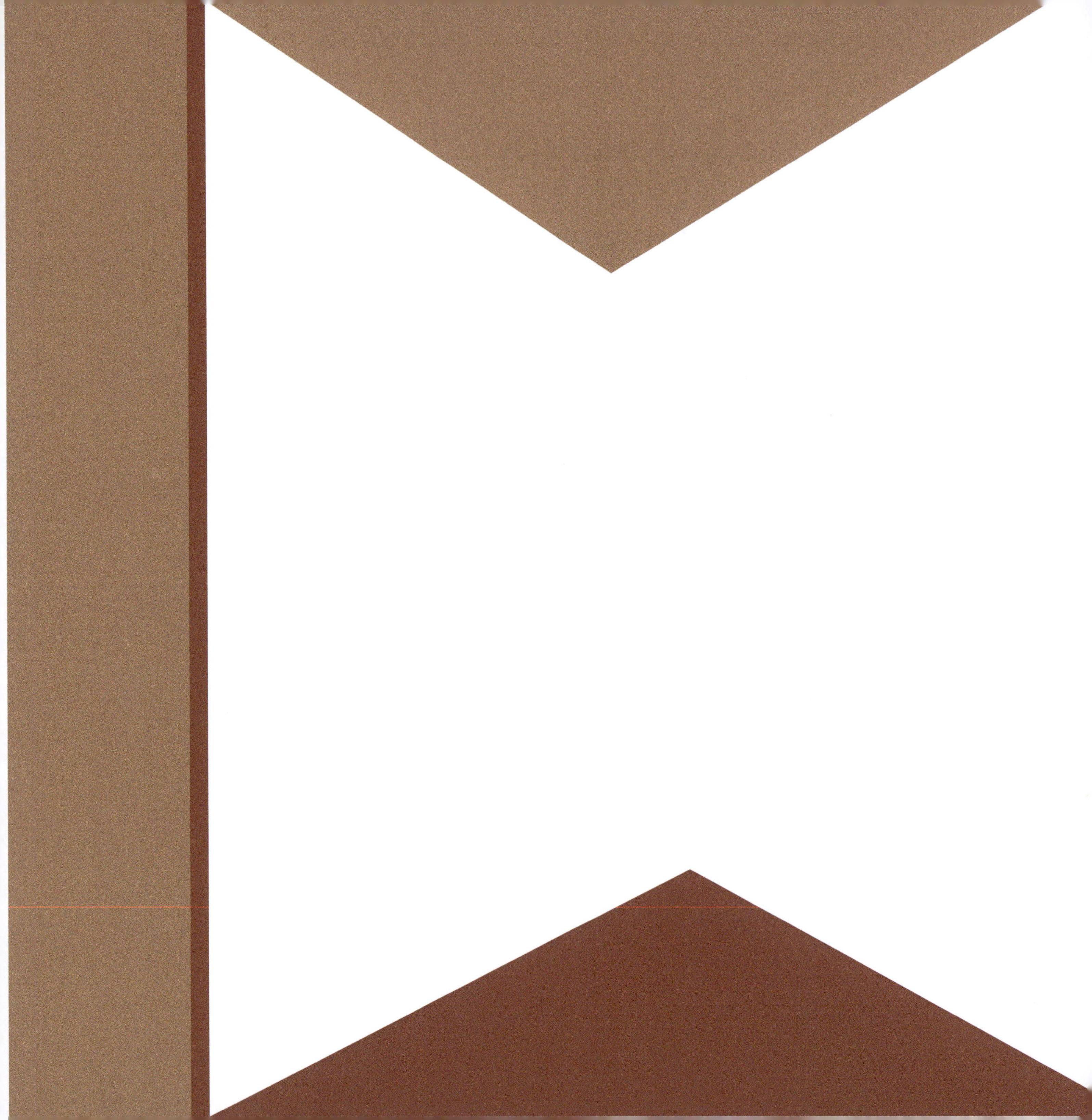

ARTS AND CULTURE: SYMBOLS AND CONCEPTS

There are symbols from all parts of the African continent: West, Central, South, North, and East. The images range from sculpture to the engraving of everyday objects through the making of mini passport masks that function like business cards. Identity (passport) masks were used in pre-colonial Central Africa (Cameroon, Kongo and Gabon) for travel and were usually made of terracotta. These items were held in the hand and could easily be stored in a pocket. Sometimes they were pierced with a hole at the top, and people would pass a string through them and wear them around the neck. The masks carried messages about the profession and social status of the holder. Those in a high position in society used only a few colors (one or two) to decorate their masks. The youth and apprentice masks featured many colors and also had different shapes. Today passport masks are used as decoration and are hung on the walls of shops or houses.

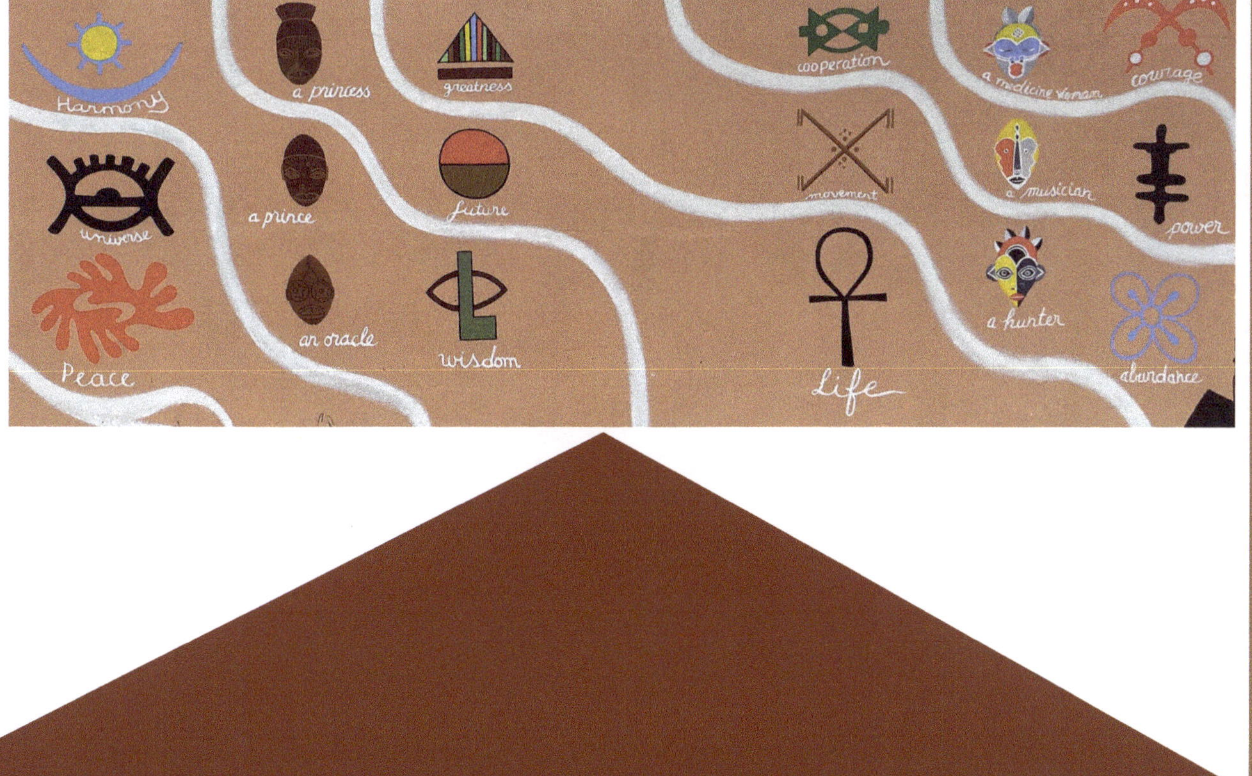

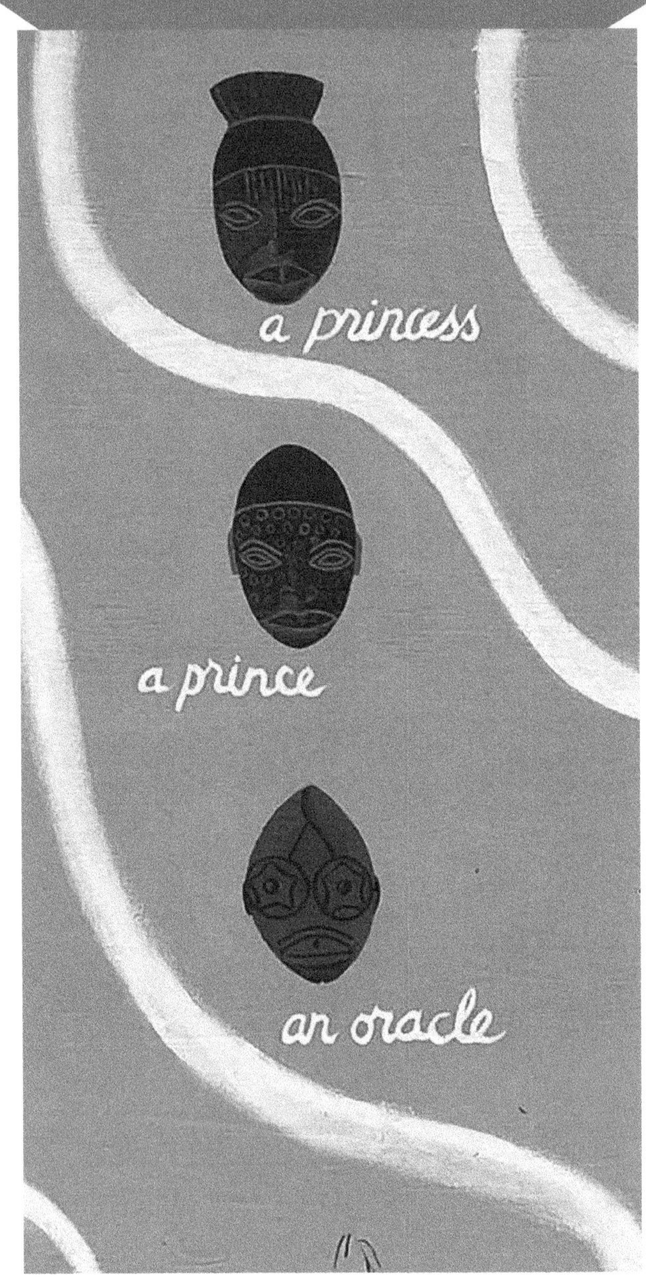

Passport Masks, Central Africa.

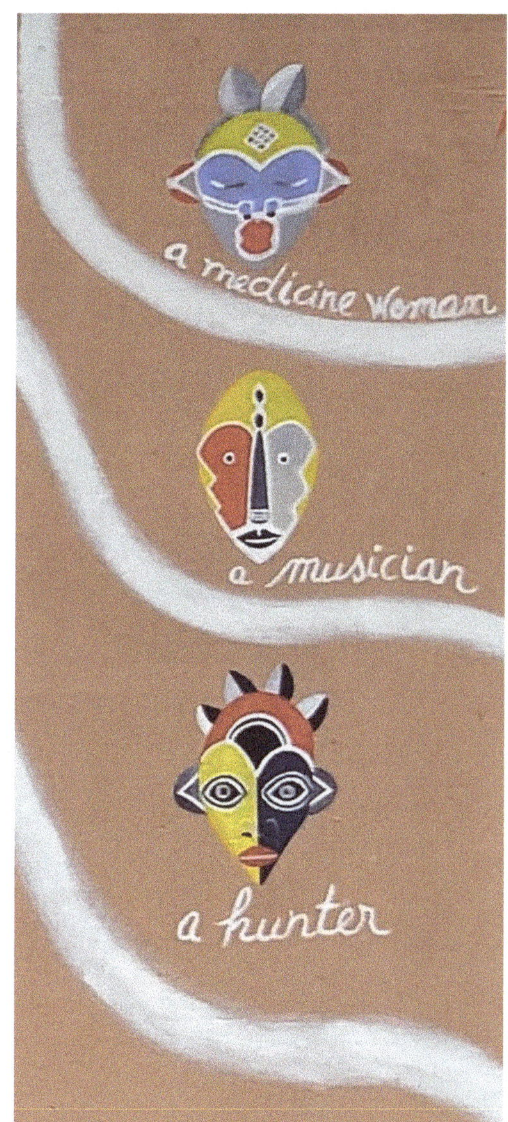

Passport Masks.

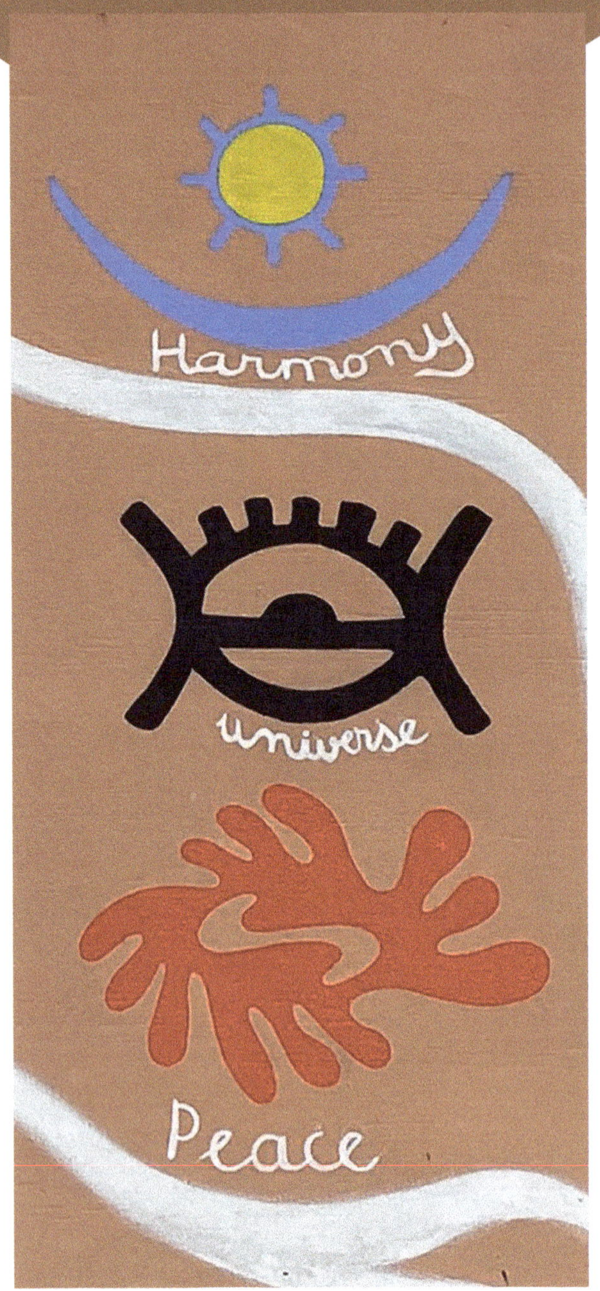

Adinkra, West Africa.

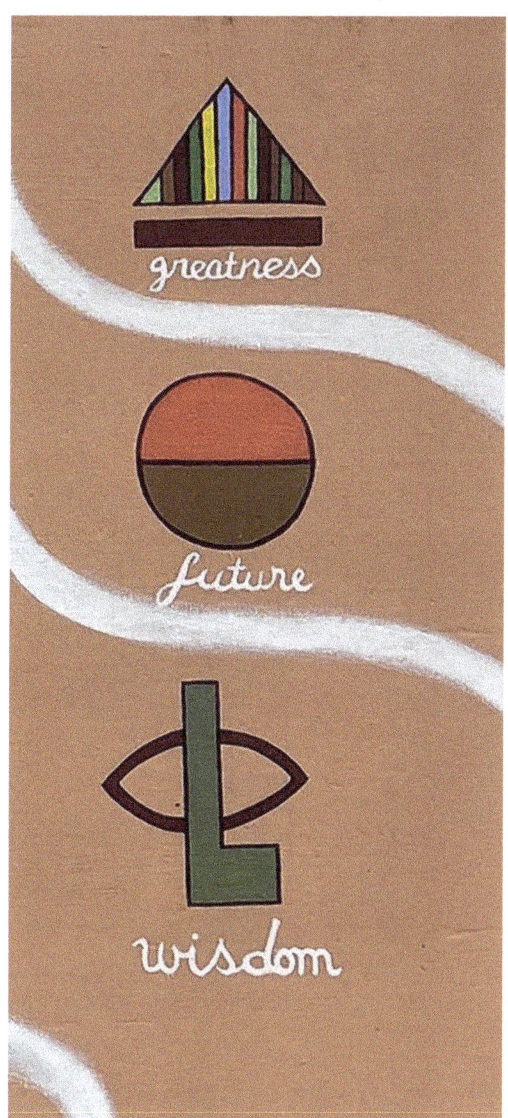

Ndebele, South Africa.

61

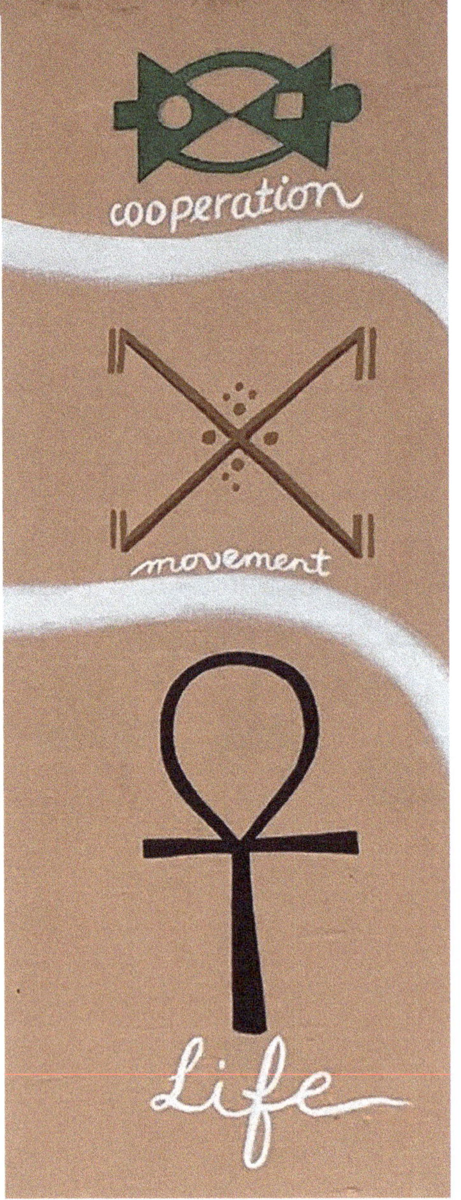

West, North, East Africa.

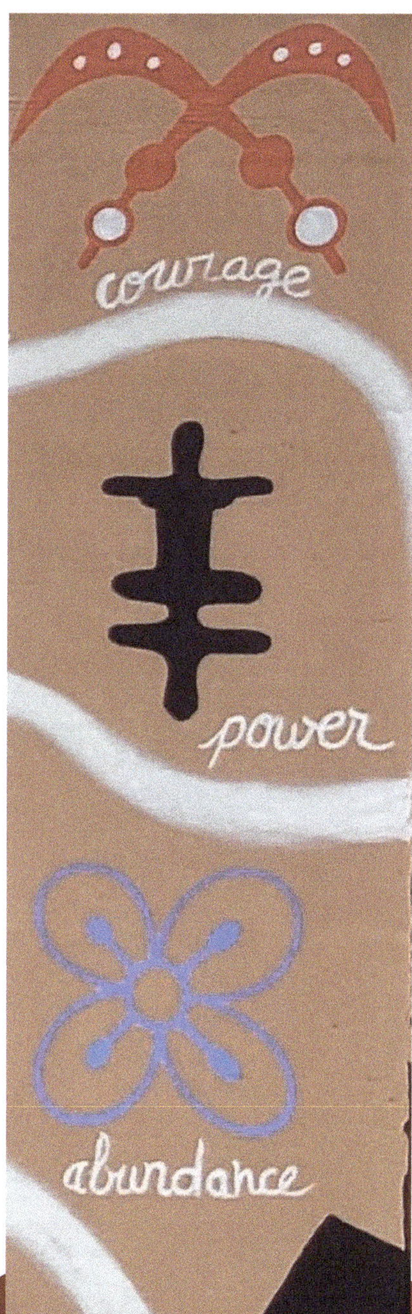

West Africa.

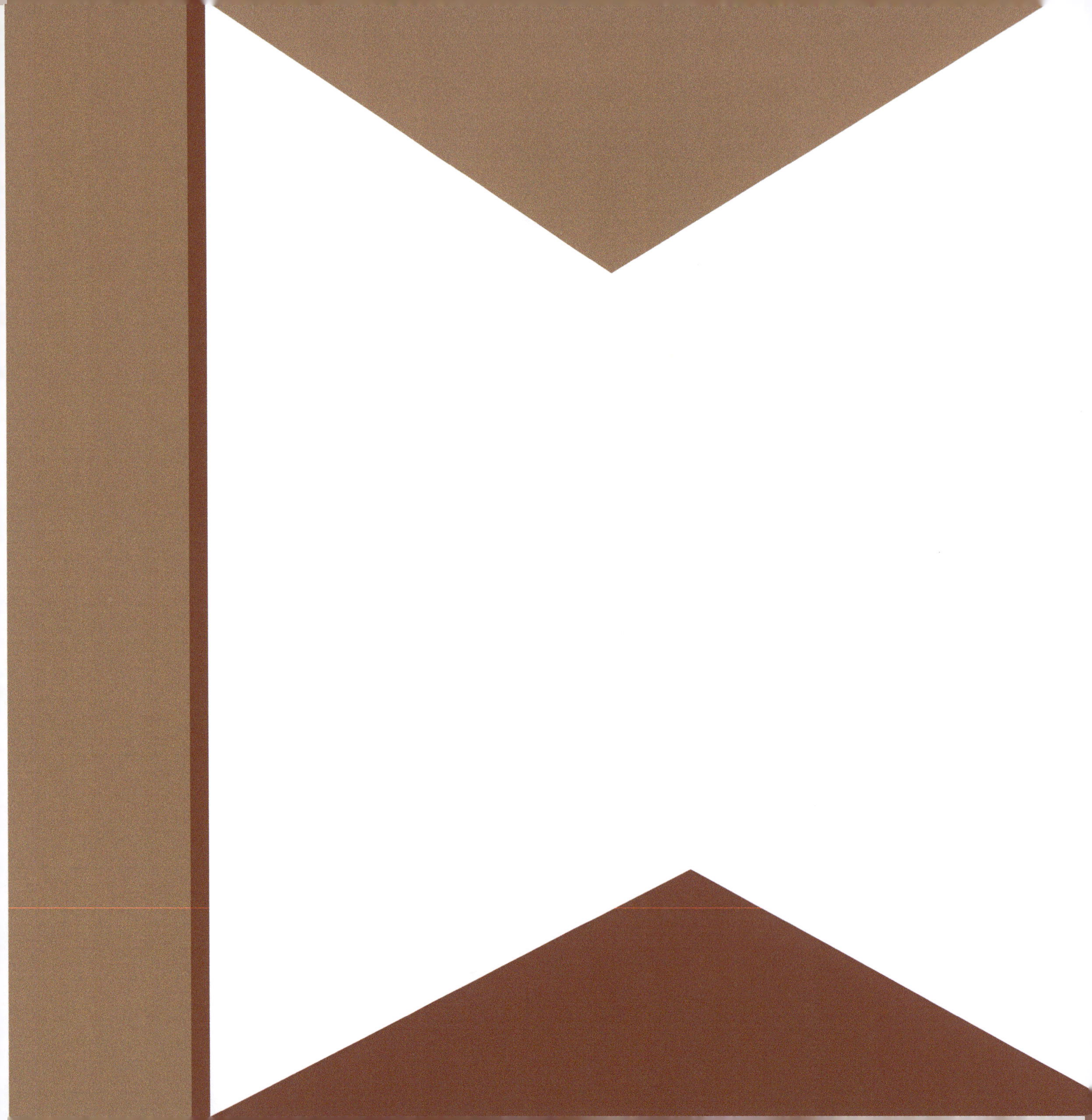

TRANSMISSION

The banana tree is a symbol of the continuity of the works of our ancestors. Therefore, it is not surprising that these plants flourish throughout Africatown.

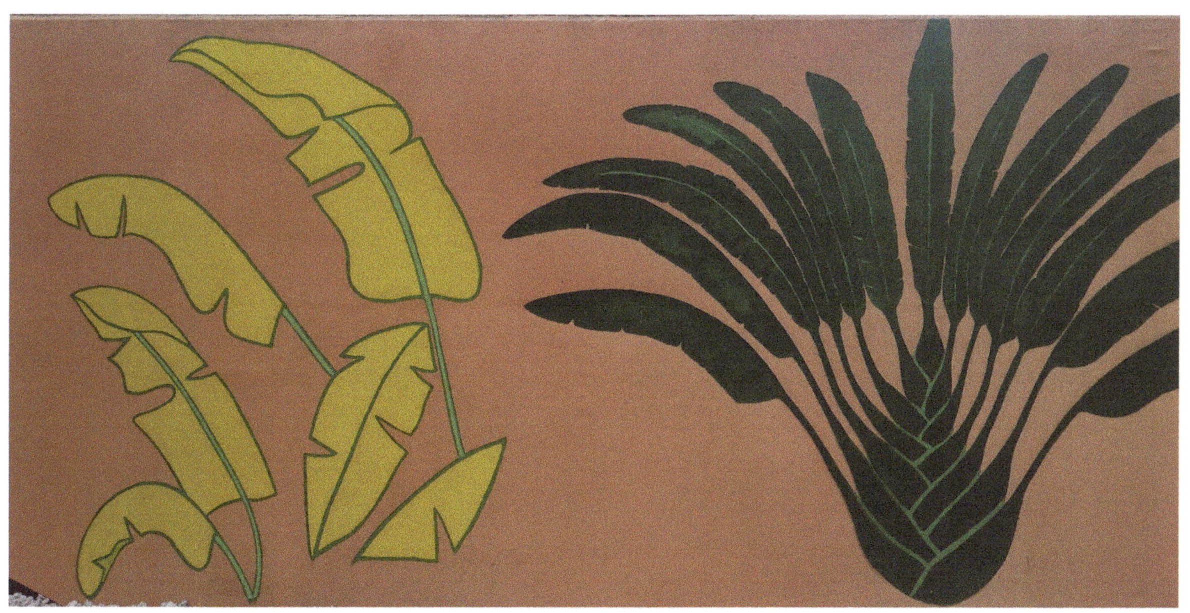

Banana trees.

The fan-shaped banana tree is called traveler's tree. It does not bear fruits. It contents water at the bottom, which allows the travelers to quench their thirst on the way.

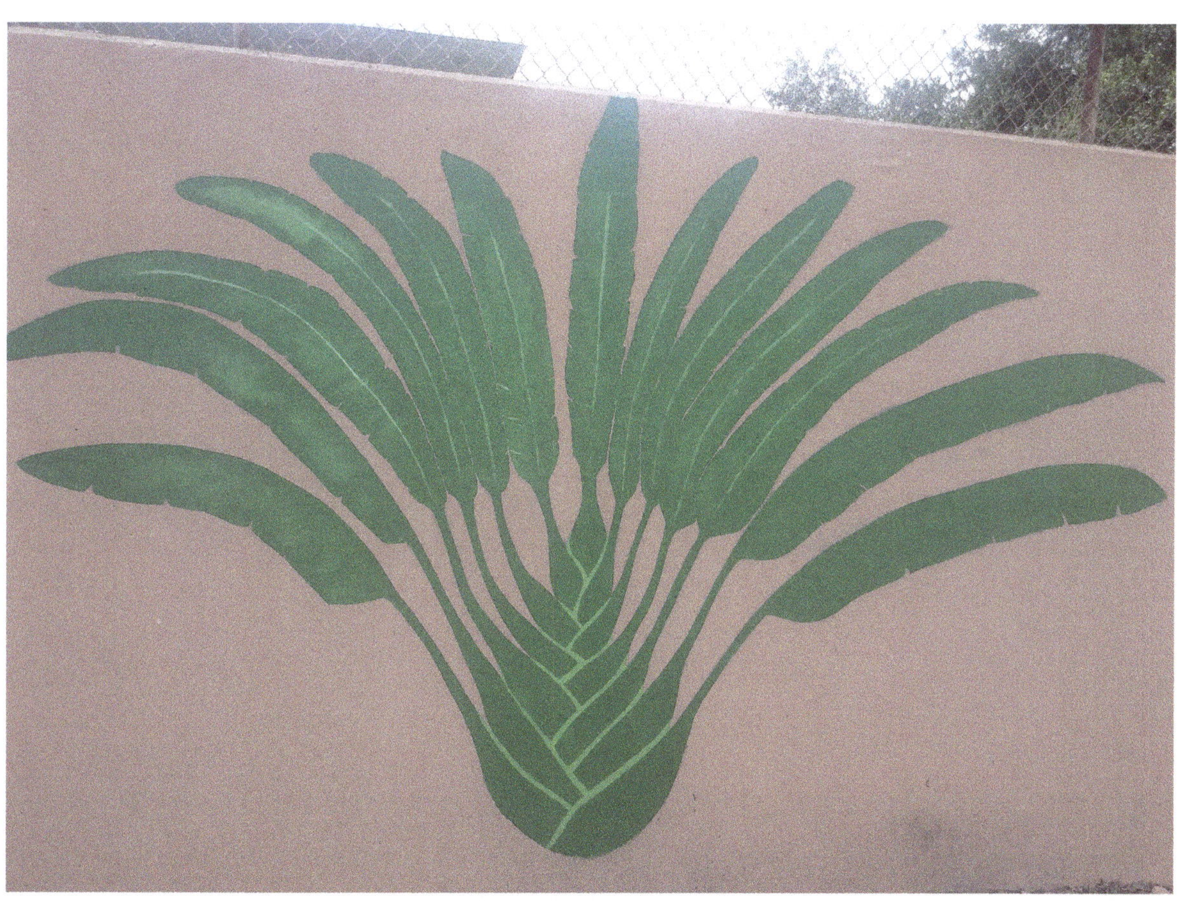

The traveler's tree

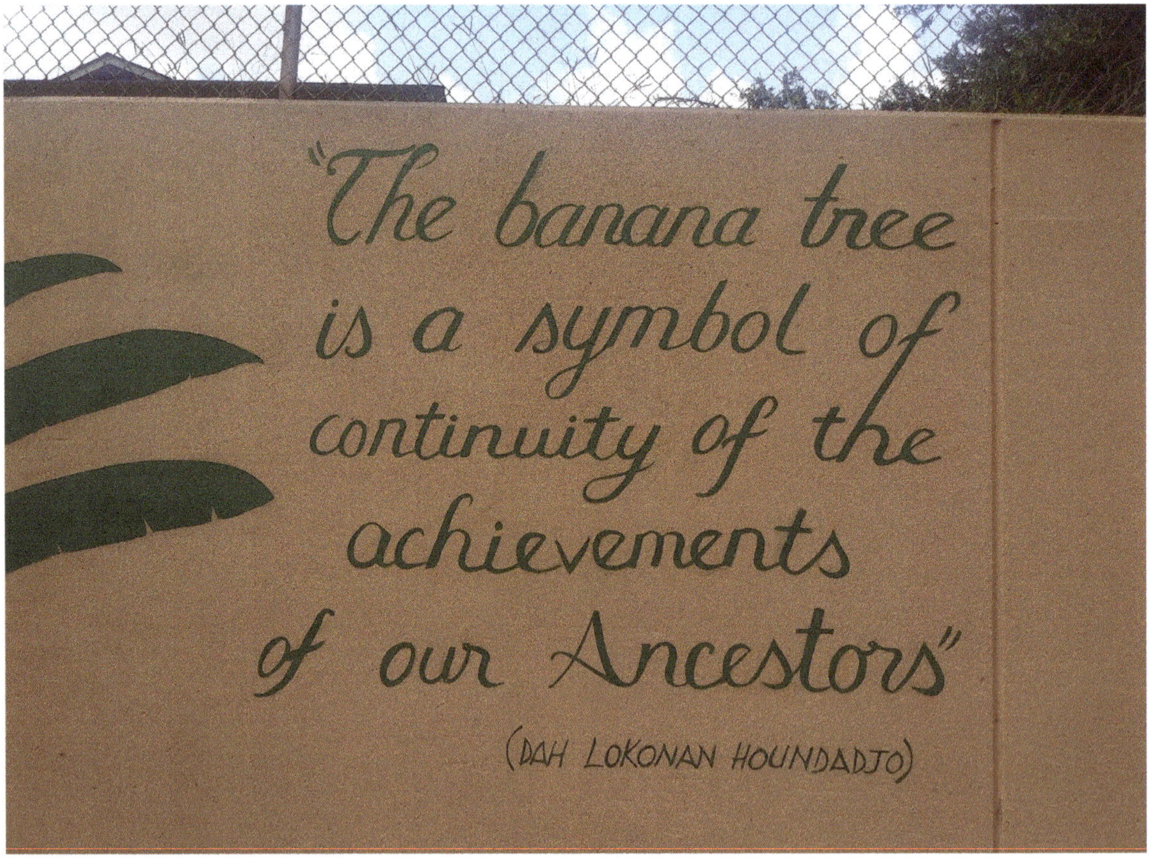

"The banana tree
is a symbol of
continuity of the
achievements
of our Ancestors"
(DAH LOKONAN HOUNDADJO)

CREDITS

Welcome to the Africatown Community! *Ngiloba* the giraffe has an eye on everything and welcomes you with kindness.

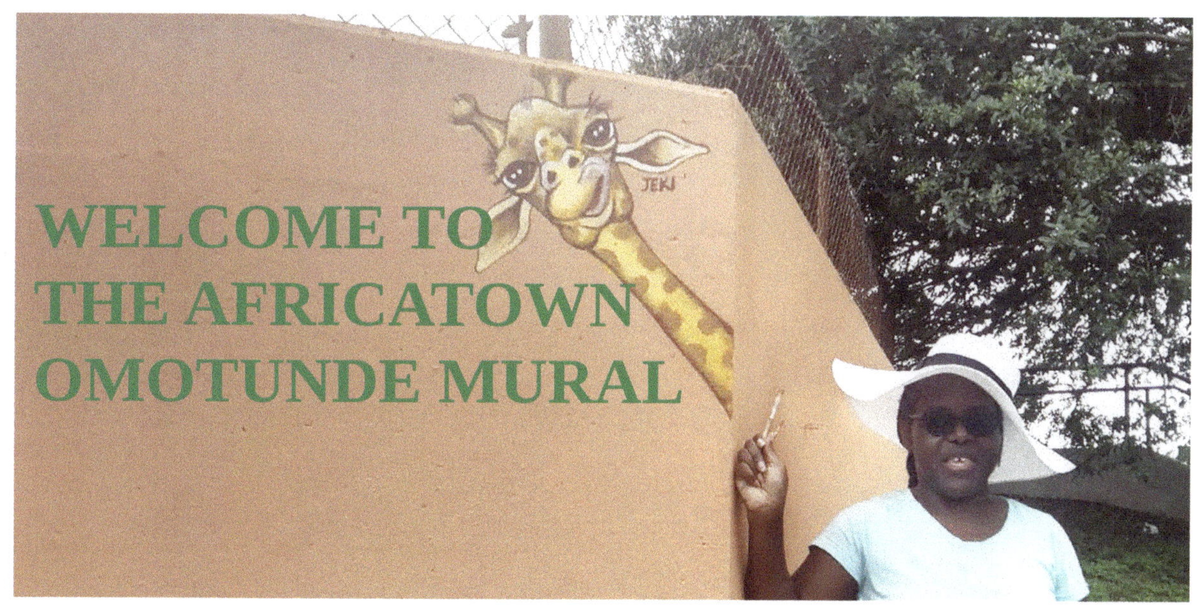

6259

We are in 6259 and soon will be in 6260 (end of July 2023)

2023+4236=6259

The year 2023 corresponds to the year 6259 of the ancient African calendar adopted in 4236 BC by the Egyptian administration. It is the oldest calendar in the world.

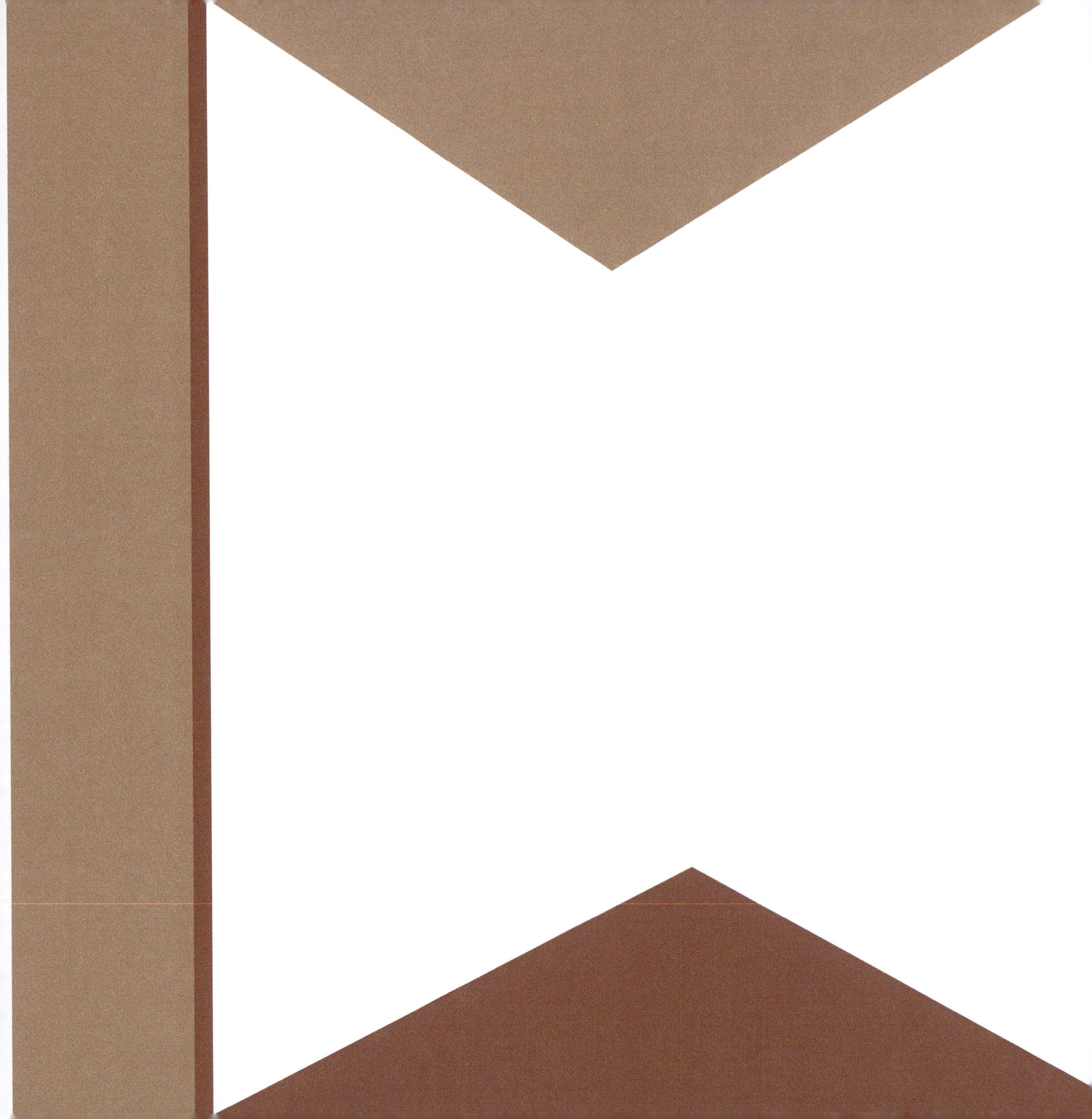

AFRICAN SCRIPTURE MAP

Africa has a large number of writing systems; these are some examples : *Adinkra, Vai, Bamum, Nsibidi, Ghez, Mandombe, Tifinagh...*

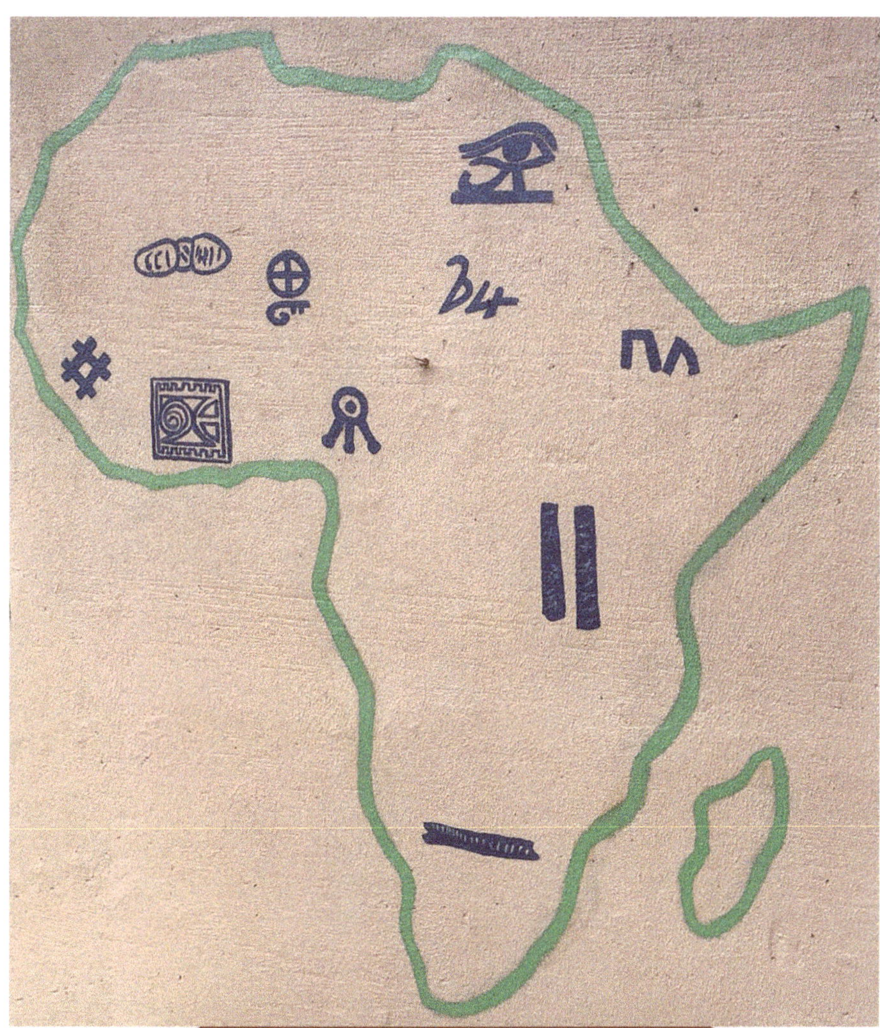

Map of some writing and calculating systems.

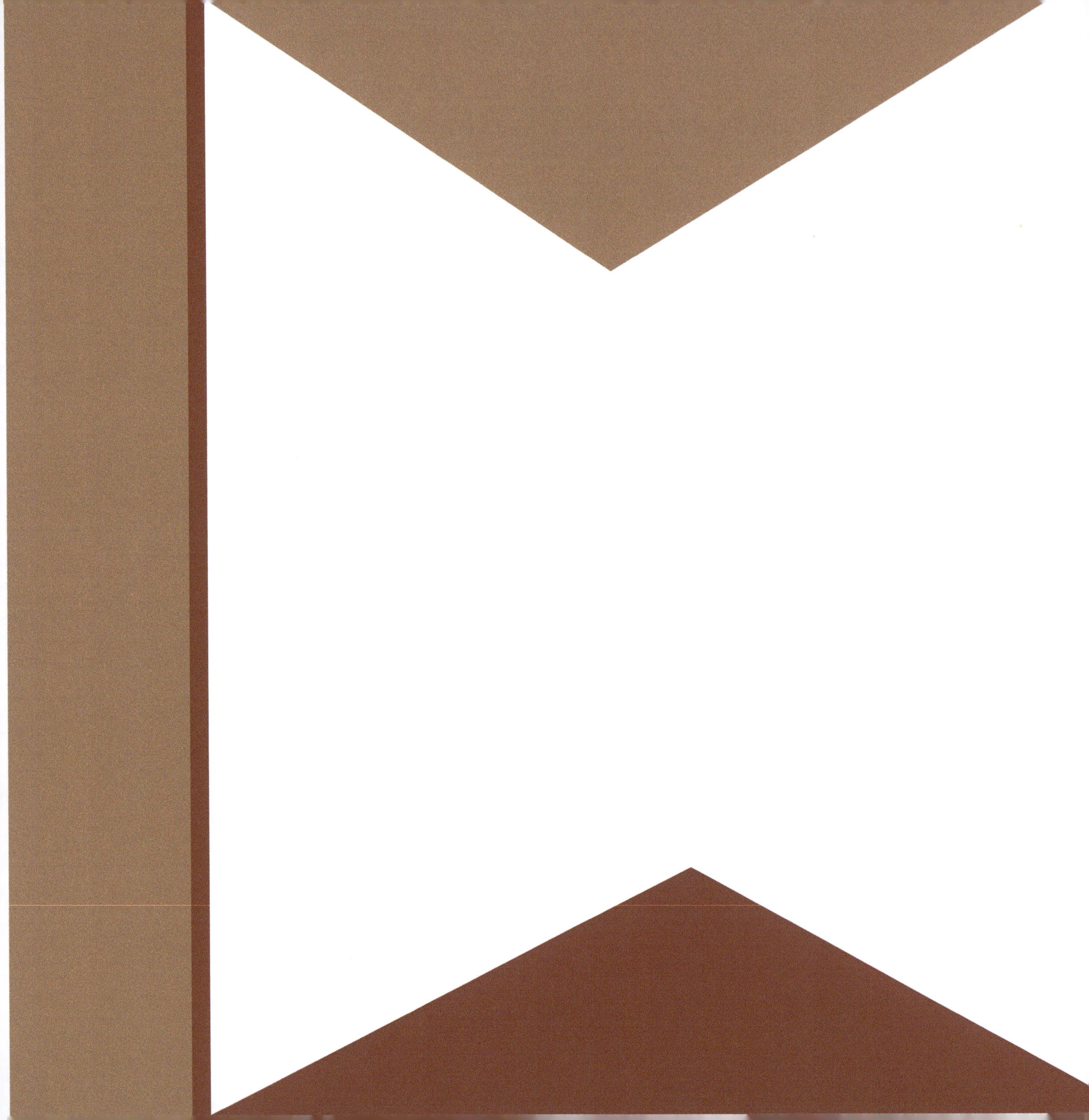

MAKING OF THE MURAL

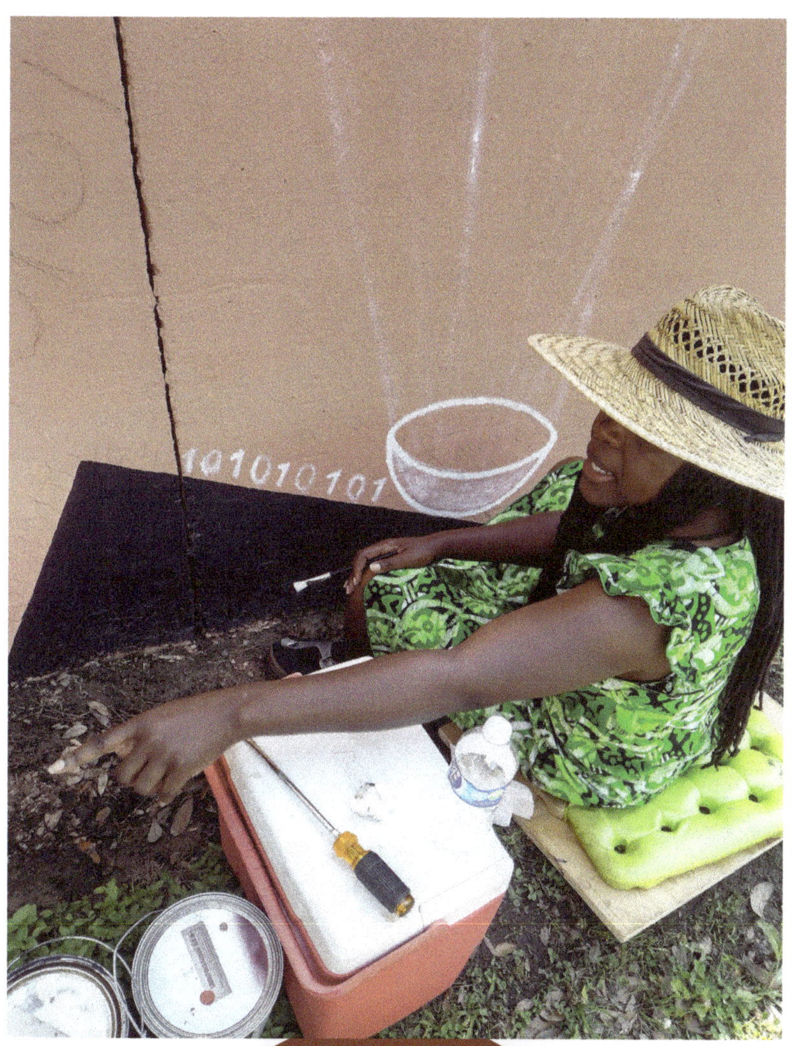

Binary code

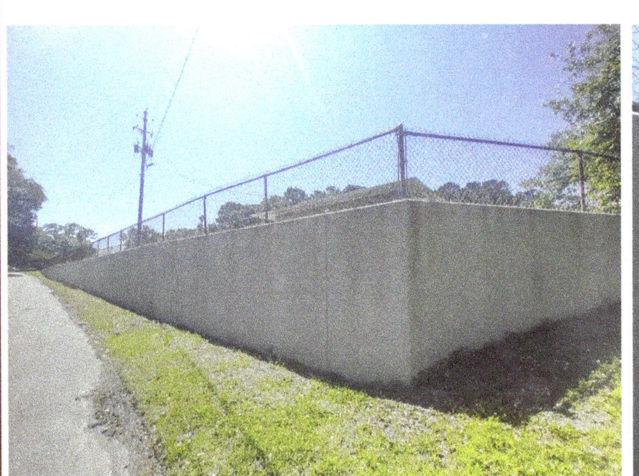

Grey wall, angle

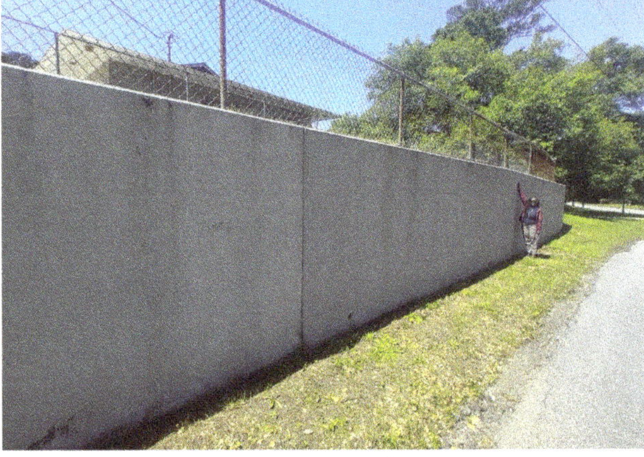

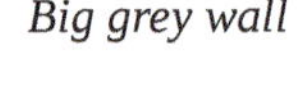

Big grey wall

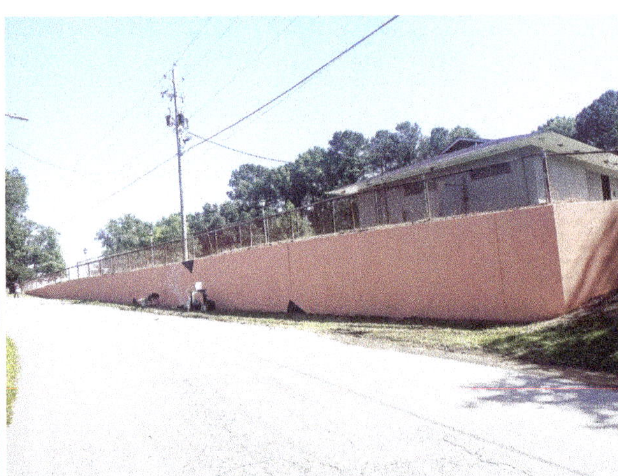

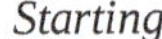

Starting

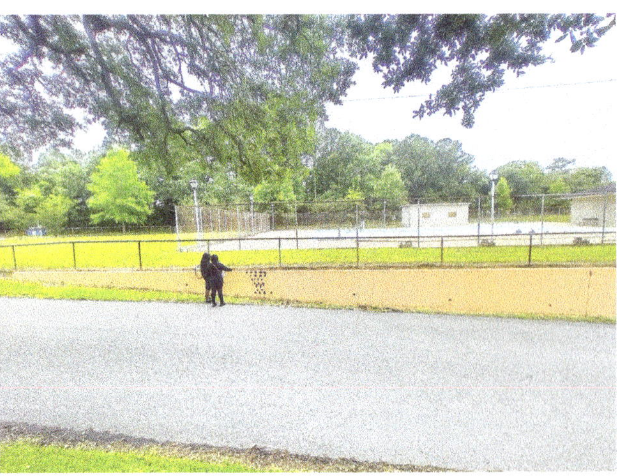

Starting kassena

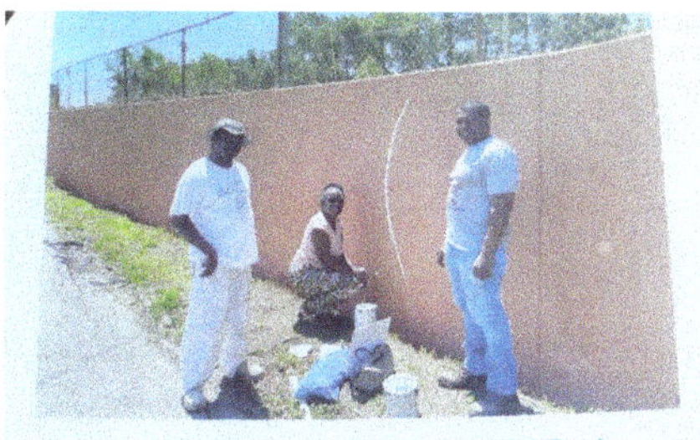

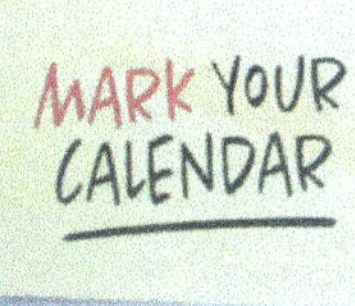

New Mural Taking Form at Kidd Park

As the famous mural of The Clotilda on Africatown Boulevard gets a fresh coat of paint, another one is taking form inside the historic Africatown Community at Kidd Park. Benin native Jeki Esso is residing in Mobile over the next year with her husband, a visiting professor at the University of South Alabama. Jeki has voluntarily undertaken to design and paint the new mural with important symbols of Africa that will not only beautify the neighborhood and park, but will also educate youth and adults alike in Africatown about their native heritage. ACDC's Charlie Williams has been assisting in the efforts.

Article

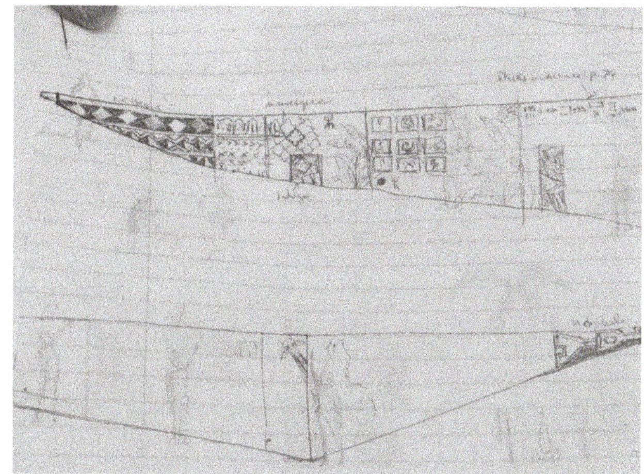

Sketch

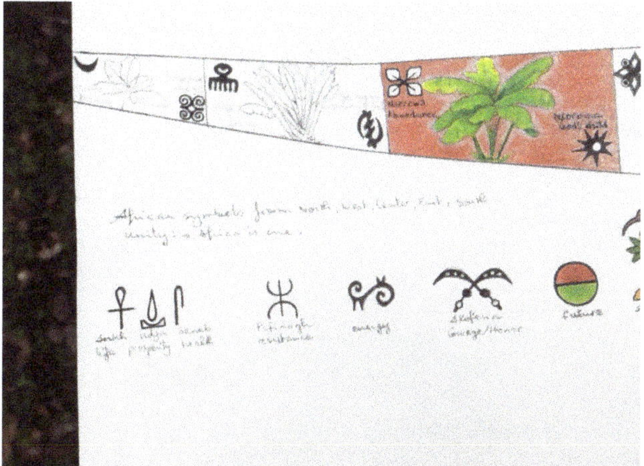

Sketch 2

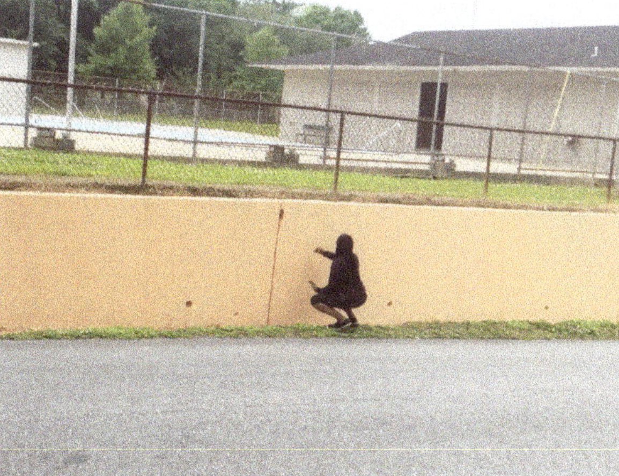

Beginning with pencil

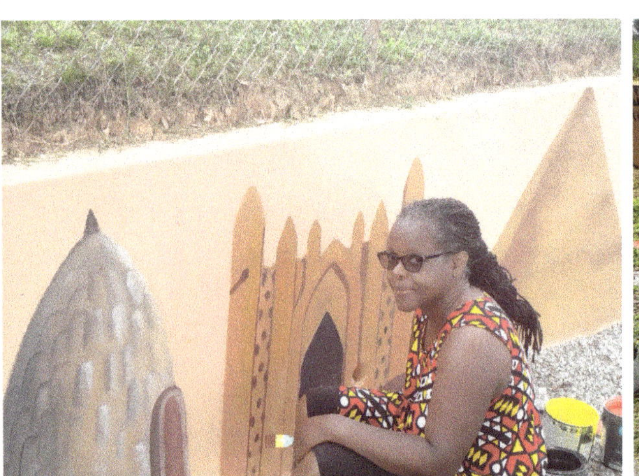

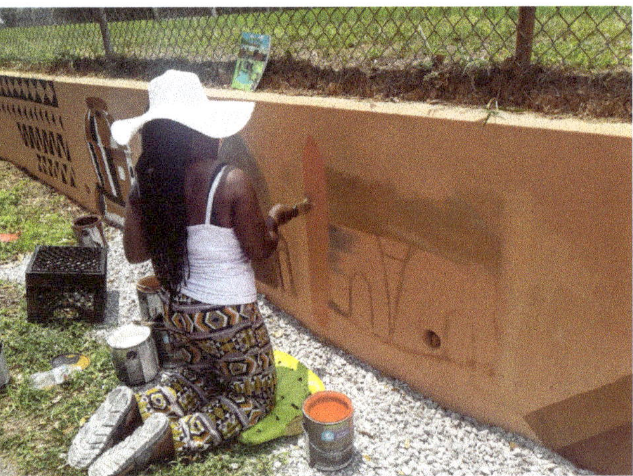

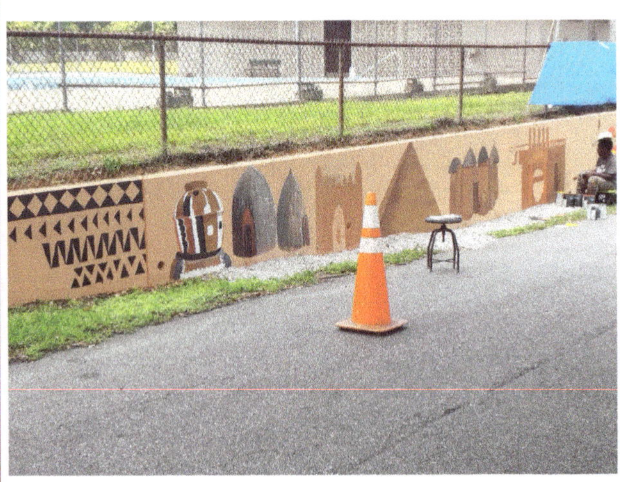

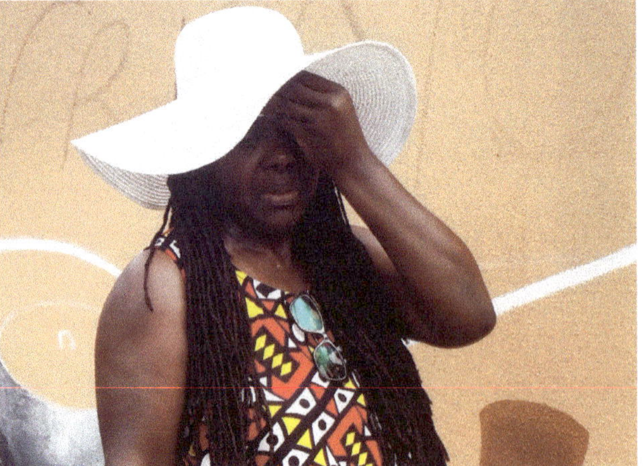

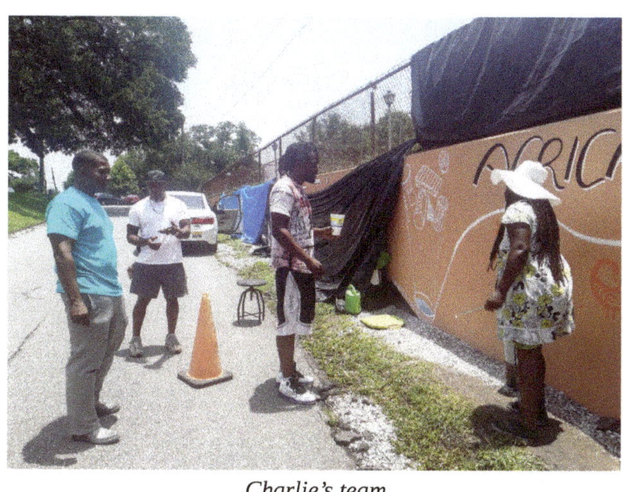

Charlie's team

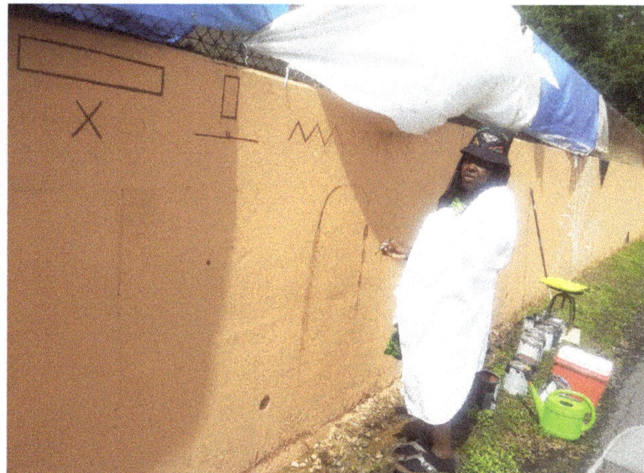

Ifa

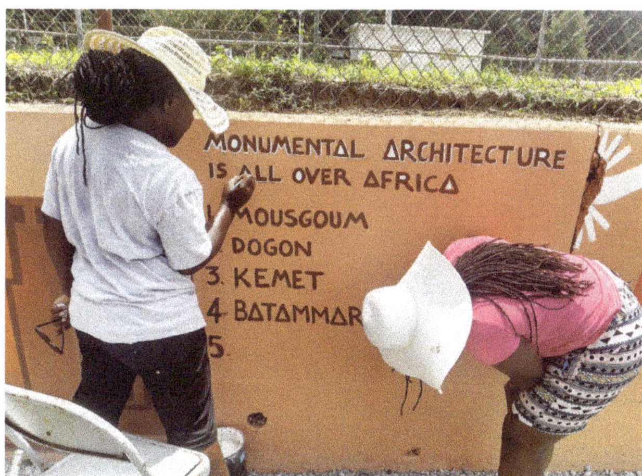

Eyala my assistant

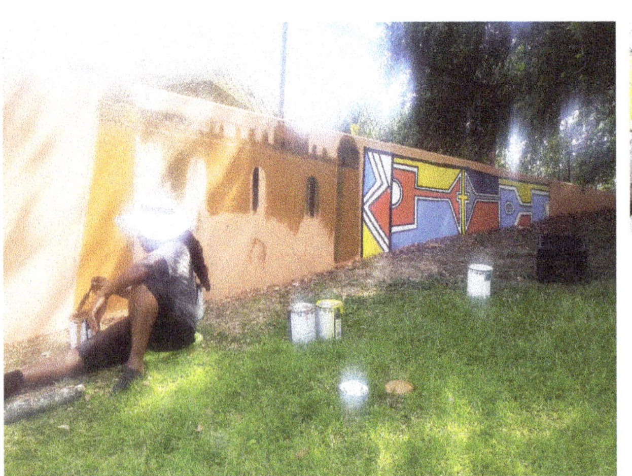

Gondar and Bugs.

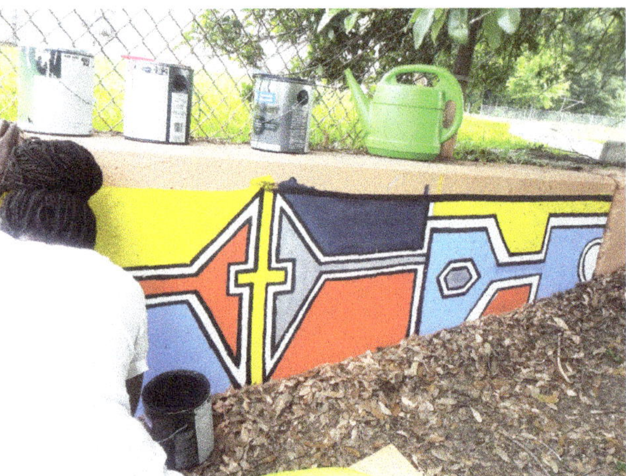

Ndebele and Bugs.

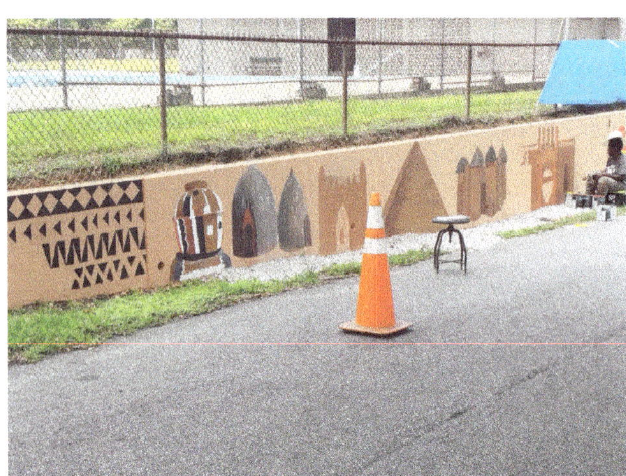

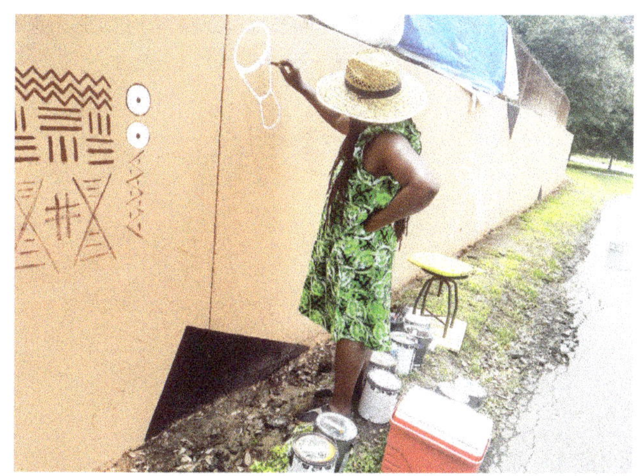

Music

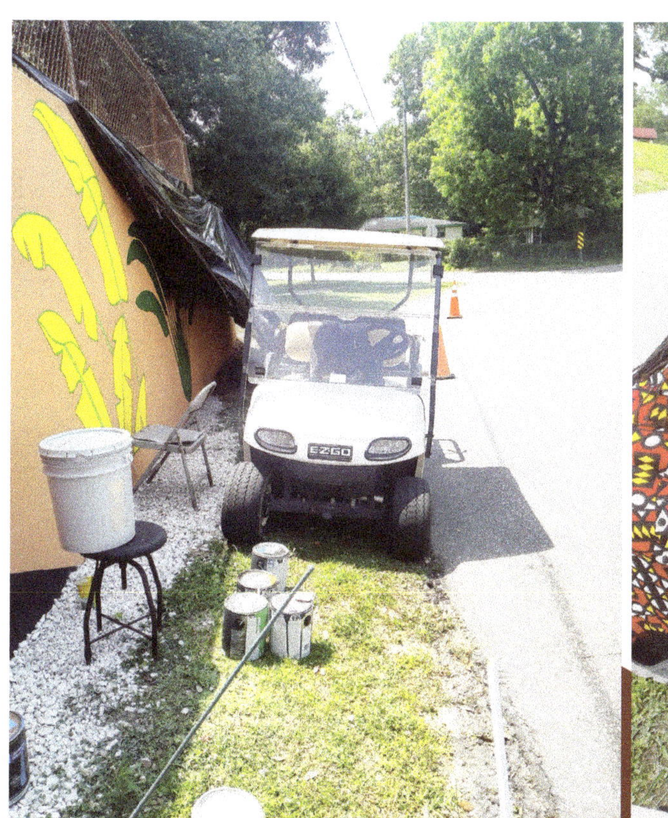

The cart

The jar

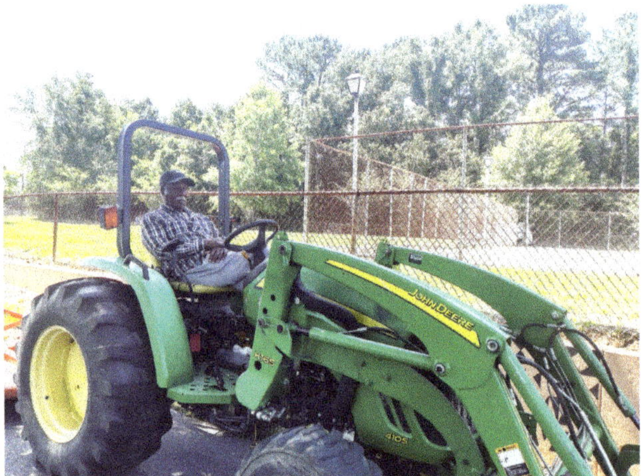

Mr Jones supervises

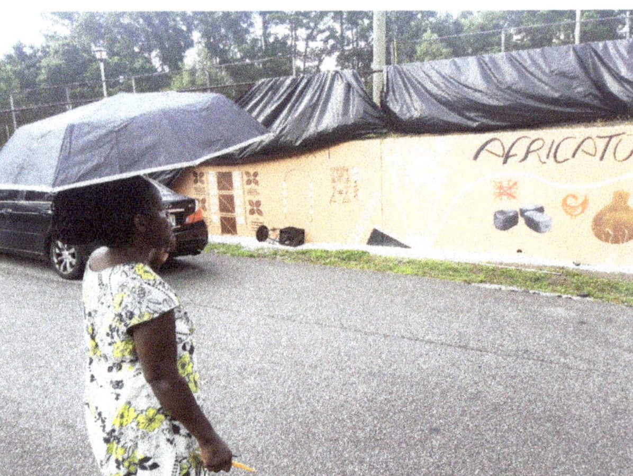

Raining

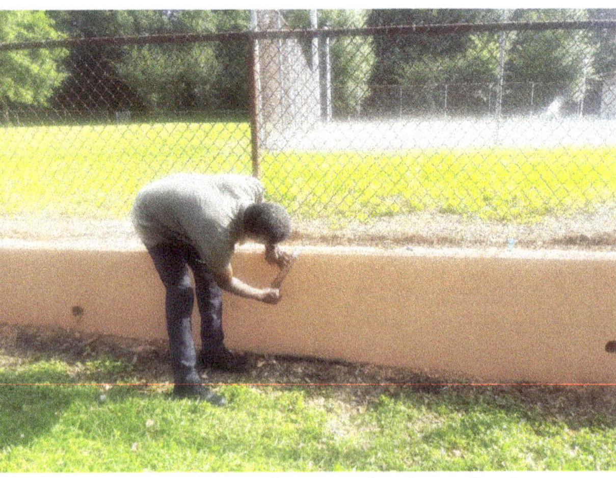

My assistant Dr Gnammankou is tracing !

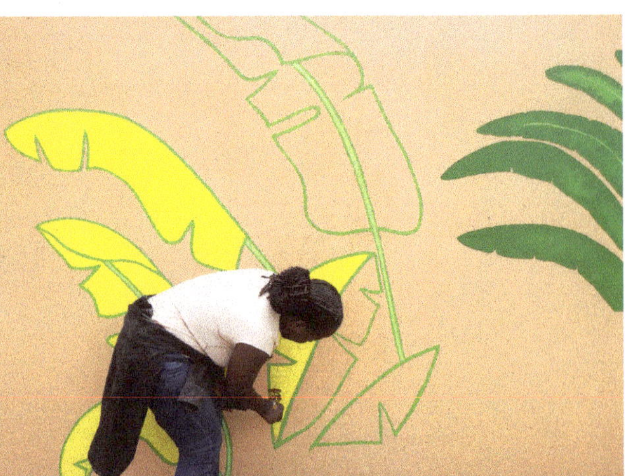

Yellow banana

VISITORS

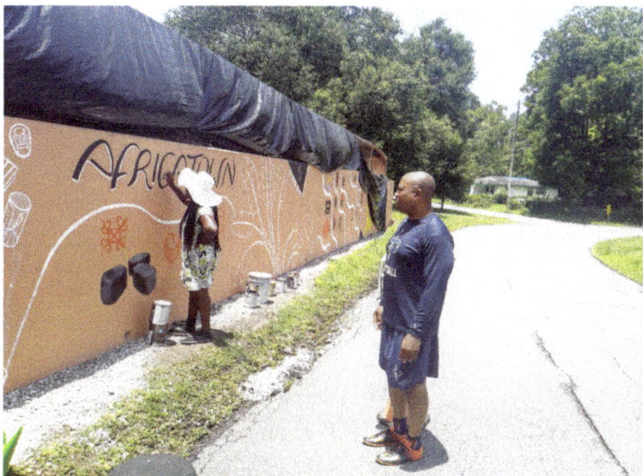

Cleon Junior

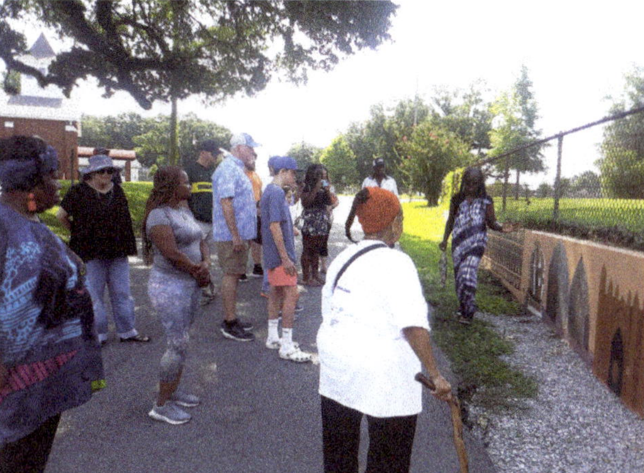

Community

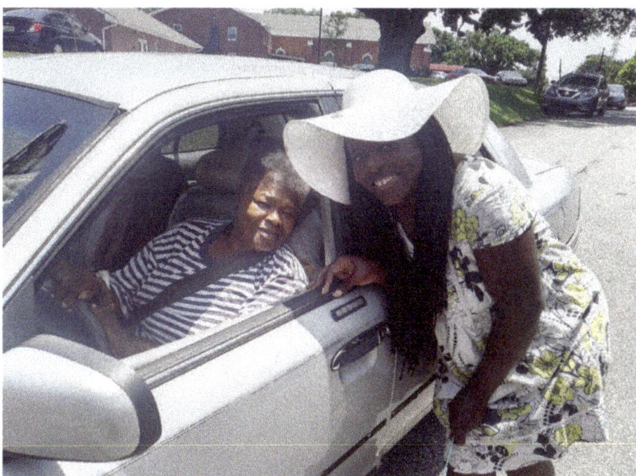

Maman Carla

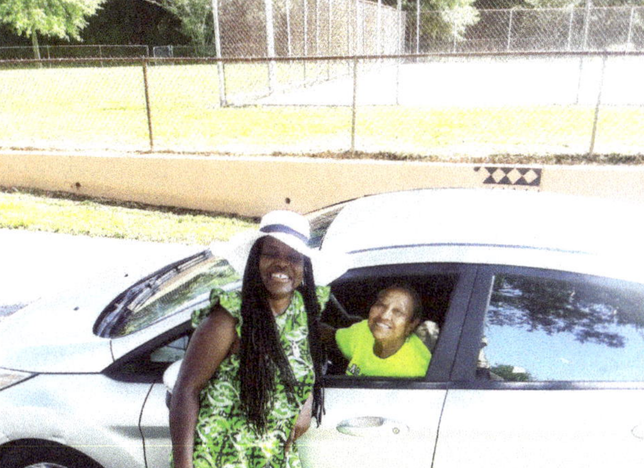

Ms Sarah Jackson

ACKNOWLEDGEMENTS

Africatown Community Development Corporation (ACDC)
Mr Cleon Jones,
Ms Angela Jones
Mr Charles Williams, Ms Rochelle Crenshaw-Williams
Mr Sydney
Mr Waynes
Mr Arthor
Mr Cleon Jones Junior
The staff of the swimming pool at Kidd Park
MCTS
The City of Mobile
Commissioner Ms Merceria Ludgood
The City of Prichard
Mayor Jimmy Gardner
Dr Kathy Cooke
Ms Kimberly Pettway
Ms Shawn Dillard
Dr Alison Blakely
Mr Robert Clopton Sr
Ms Ruth Ballard
Rev Christopher L Williams Sr
Ms Elizabeth Smith-Incer
Mr Ramsey Sprague
Ms Janice Rinne
Dr Christine Rinne
Mr Daniel Lopez

Ms and Mr Karlos Finley
Dr Afia Zakiya
Dr Irma McClaurin
Ms Connie Fredericks-Malone,
Dr Jim Malone
Ms Lorna Woods
Ms Ouida Shears
Mrs Thelma Maïben-Owens
Ms Carla Varner-Rigsby
Ms Debra
Ms Jacqueline Tunstall
Fulbright SIR Programs
IIE Suzan Muendl,
Claire Winter
Natalie Rehberger
Dr Julie Taylor
Ms Sarah Jackson
Mr Tony Orlando
Mr Kojo John Bacot
Ms Joycelyn Davis
Ms Louise Mbella
Dr Veronique Helenon
Ms Laurie Hunter
Dr Pat Frazier
Mrs Vickii Howell
Darron Paterson
Dr Joel Billingsley
Dr Marsha Hamilton
Dr Joy Washington
Dr Dave Messenger
Dr Patrick Houessou

Dr Patrick Effiboley
Dr Mara Kozelsky
Dr Harrison Miller
Dr Bri Ard
Ms Jen Knutson
Dr Kern Jackson
Dr Susan Mc Cready
Dr Susan Fitzsimmons
Dr Simon Grelet
Dr Mihaela Marin
Dr Ellen Harrington
Mr Maurice Chavarry
Ms Maureena Walker
Ms Marie-Christine Whitman
Ms Carla Saint-Paul
Ms Claire Whitman
Ms Isabelle Whitman
Mr Alex Saint-Paul
Dr Clayton Vaughn-Roberson
Ms/Mr Mary and Jim Mather

I am grateful for everything you've done.

A special thanks to the whole Africatown Community
Unity, Reconnection, Rebirth !
One love!

Jeki

Afterword: African Art is Forever

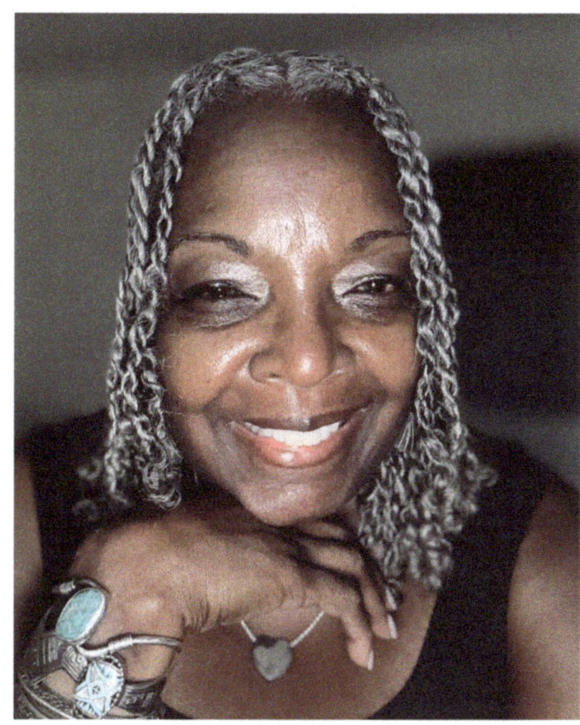

Afterword: African Art is Forever

Fifty years from now, when people stand at the Africatown *Omotunde* mural, they will want to know the who, the how, and the why.

Who?

The Benin-Cameroon artist, Jeki (Joelle) Esso, aka Jeki, has created a visual time capsule. Using pictograms, symbols, patterns, mathematical equations, words in African languages, renderings of African architecture, and colors, she invites the viewer to cross historic, cultural, linguistic, geographical, philosophical, and even ideational boundaries.

In an interview I did with her, Jeki, gave the following response to my query about one very prominent image in the mural: "why the banana tree and banana leaves?"

Jeki: *Because, the banana tree is a symbol of transmission from generation to generation. And, I think it is a good symbol for Africatown" (https:// bit.ly/Africatownmural).*

Viewers in the present are now connected with Africa's past through the artwork of Jeki Esso, and can see how ancient elements and structures are also reflected in modern African art, architecture, and science.

The end result is clear evidence that African Art is Forever!

How?

The viewer of this mural does not need to speak or know a specific African language to experience the breadth of Africa's impact on the world and recognize the magnificence of Africa's "monumental" architecture, its contributions to mathematics, science, art, and symbolic thinking, all reflected in the Africatown mural that Jeki has designed, now permanently displayed outdoors in Africatown Plateau, Alabama.

Realistically, many Africatown residents will *never* be able to travel to the continent of Africa. They will never hear its multiplicity of languages or experience the diversity of the continent's many unique cultures that infuse the various groups of people who are all African—yet different.

This mural is a reminder and testimony that, after all, Africa is not a country, it is a continent!

As such, it is comprised of many different kinds of people who have distinct cultures, different languages, their own worldviews, belief systems, art forms, religions, and diverse histories—some of which go back further than others.

The people of Africatown may never know that even within each African nation-state (kingdom) there sometimes existed multiple ethnic groups or tribal affiliations. In modern times, some of these internal cultural and ethnic differences have led to horrific present-day conflicts—such as the Rwanda genocide (1994) or the country of Liberia's two civil wars (1989-1997 and 1993-2003), or modern-day slavery/human trafficking in the Sudan, which the U.S. State Department estimates has created a refugee population of 800,000 in 2021.

It was such conflicts, as well as pressure from early colonizers like the Portuguese, that led to African kingdoms participating in the enslavement enterprise. In a 2023 lecture in Africatown, Benin Fulbright Scholar at the University of South Alabama, Dr. Dieudonné Gnammankou, (see preface), provided insights and additional historical contexts for why African nations might have been involved in the slave trade.

His research suggests that slaves (often war captives) were able to become full citizens of African kingdoms after a limited period of servitude. Thus, Africans' understanding of "slavery" differed vastly from Europeans—and who knows if the type of slavery captives would endure was fully grasped by African kings when they sold war captives, though rarely anyone from their own kingdoms. They needed to sacrifice a few for the greater good—we know of only *one* captive on the slave ship *Clotilda* that came from Dahomey.

Thanks to Kossola, who described his capture to Black anthropologist, Zora Neale Hurston, we have a vivid account of how people were captured in order to be sold as slave. His description of the Dahomey women soldiers who raided his village, killed many, and captured some to sell as slaves, is vivid, and decades after the event, still painful for him to recount. (Visit: *Clotilda: The Exhibition* (*https://clotilda.com/*, Africatown Heritage House: A Site of the History Museum of Mobile).

The involvement of African kings in the slave trade is a counter narrative that many whites like to throw in the faces of those who critique the industry of slavery. However, we must remember, Africa is a continent, not a country. At the time of the slave trade, it was comprised of numerous kingdoms and chiefdoms, many of which were engaged in ongoing internal conflicts. The African involvement in the slave trade was not the continent's finest hour.

However, we must not judge the past too harshly from the perspective of the present. It helps to view the decisions African kings and chiefs made back then through a modern lens of historical pragmatism. Those sold for slaves were viewed as enemies and war captives and not the king's or chief's own people. More often than not, these leaders sold their enemies to protect their own people, and also to gain a military advantage using access to new types of weapons like guns and canons. The Portuguese exploited this need for new weaponry, and used it as a bargaining chip— new types of weapons would be sold, but only in exchange for slaves. .

What Africatown also has learned from Dr. Gnammankou's lectures was that there was far more resistance by African kingdoms than complicity. Another hidden fact he revealed was that many African kingdoms and chiefdoms had absolutely no involvement in the slave trade and actively resisted the enslavement of any people as best they could against guns and cannons. While those that did participate and sold their enemies and sometimes used a quota system that capped the number of people who could be taken as slaves.

Still other kingdoms, like the Congo, vigorously resisted, and were destroyed for their audacity to rise up against Portuguese slavers, backed by military ships sometimes. Dr. Gnammankou's research of original Portuguese documents confirmed the massacre of over 1,000 people in the Kingdom of the Congo and its destruction. As punishment for refusal to participate in the slave trade and taking military actions, the Portuguese decimated the Kingdom of the Congo—killing the king, generals, priests, and anyone of noble birth who might provide leadership. This left the chiefdoms, villages, and the people, once united under the Congo's rule, without leadership or protection. Overtime the Kingdom of Dahomey was established to once again unite this same area and bring leadership and protection.

In viewing the *Omotunde* mural, visitors will want to take note of the huge banana tree leaves. But you should also know that there are banana trees scattered across the landscape in Africatown and their presence will surprise visitors as they wander, and wonder, through the streets of this place filled with histories and memories (good and bad).

The existence of banana trees in Africatown reflect the ancestral presence of those who came before the Descendants and current resident; those who came before not only planted the banana trees, but also left other signs and symbols of Africa carved in ironwork on some of the windows of houses in Africatown or in the shape of roofs, and in the stories (rememories) they handed down to their Descendants.

Why?

In my opinion, the reason why Jeki Esso has designed this mural is for it to serve as a visible symbol of contemplation, resilience, resistance, and connections. It is intended to provoke contemplation, instruct the unenlightened, facilitate reflection about the African roots of Africatown and the African American diaspora, and remind us about the veracity of what the continent of Africa has contributed to the artistic, intellectual, scientific, mathematical development of the world—centuries before Europeans. It is evidence of our humanity as Africans and African Americans.

But mostly, through her art, Jeki has shared a bit of herself, her country, her worldview, her creativity as an African woman artist, with us, her kinfolk, in the United States.

Sawubona (We See You) | Yebo Sawubona (Yes, We See You Too) [https://youtu.be/2IjUkVZRPK8]

 Irma McClaurin, PhD/Soc St.D./MFA

Irma McClaurin (https://linktr.ee/dr.irma) is an activist Black Feminist anthropologist, a past president of Shaw (Raleigh North Carolina), and has held numerous other leadership positions. McClaurin completed the MFA in English and the PhD in Anthropology from the University of Massachusetts Amherst, and was just awarded the Honorary Doctorate of Social Studies by her alma mater, Grinnell College in 2023. McClaurin is also the founder of the Irma McClaurin Black Feminist Archive, located at UMass, and an award-winning author and poet. Her book *Black Feminist Anthropology: Theory, Politics, Praxis and Poetics* was named an "Outstanding Academic Title" in 2002 and the Black Press of America selected her as "Best in the Nation Columnist" in 2015. She won the Gwendolyn Brooks Award in poetry in 1974. Today McClaurin is the sole proprietor of Irma McClaurin Solutions, a consulting firm, and is the Culture and Education Editor for *Insightnews.com.* A prolific writer, McClaurin has published editorials, academic articles and book chapters as well as poetry. She currently divides her time between Mobile, AL and Raleigh, NC, and is a member of the newly established Center for Diaspora and Migration Studies at the University of Liberia.